In the Name of Allah, the
Gracious, the Merciful

ISLAM & INTEREST

by
Mohammad Shafi

ISLAM & INTEREST

CONTENTS

- Prefaces
1 What is *Ar-Riba*?
2 Islam and Bank Interest - I
3 Islam and Bank Ineterst - II
4 A Model Islamic Bank
5 An Individual Sans Ar-Riba
6 Examples of Ar-Riba
7 Ahaadeeth on Ar-Riba – I
8 Ahaadeeth on Ar-Riba – II
9 Ahaadeeth on Ar-Riba – III
10 Ahaadeeth on Ar-Riba – IV
11 Insurance and Copyright
- Appendix – I
- Appendix – II
- Appendix – III
- Appendix – IV

ISLAM & INTEREST

All rights reserved by the Author.

ISLAM & INTEREST

PREFACE TO THE FIRST EDITION

Since the very early years of my adult life, I have been bothered by the general belief among Muslims that interest taken or given by Banks, or by any other institution or individual, is prohibited (*haraam*). I was aware that, despite this belief, Muslims did make interest-based transactions without any apparent feeling of guilt. Only a very few had that absolute touch-me-not attitude towards interest. Were not then most of the Muslims hypocrites on that account, I wondered. I did read the Qur'aan with English and Urdu translations, but this did not help mitigate the uneasiness in my mind in this regard. The translations equated the *Riba* that the Qur'aan prohibits with interest or usury.

It was much later in my life that it began to dawn on me that the rendering of the Qur'aanic concept of *Riba* as interest, or even usury, may not be correct. It was initially a vague idea, which gradually consolidated into conviction

ISLAM & INTEREST

after much thought and pondering over relevant verses of the Qur'aan, which I chanced to come across during my readings of the Holy Book. I have now been able to put these thoughts and ponderings into this booklet, only after the search engine in Ibrahim Shafi's Islamic Page on the Internet helped me get together all the Qur'aanic verses on *Riba*. It is a fine Page, full of information on Islam. May Allah richly reward the makers of that Page. Amen!

I wrote the chapters in this booklet initially with the intention of publishing them as separate articles. The chapters therefore have a mutually independent character; that is, a reader can read any of the chapters independently without reading the preceding chapters. It was only after writing the first three or four chapters that I decided to publish them all together in the form of a booklet. But I have tried to maintain the independent character of each chapter, so that one may, if one wants to, read any of the chapters first, and understand it completely,

ISLAM & INTEREST

without any compelling need to refer to the earlier chapters. Still, I would like the readers to read the booklet in the chronological order of the chapters to get a complete Qur'aanic concept of *Riba*.

Lastly, I wish it to be clearly understood that what is sacrosanct and cannot be questioned by us, humans, are Allah's commandments and words of advice, communicated to us by His Apostle (peace be upon him). But some of His words have been given more than one - often mutually incompatible - interpretation by different commentators. The interpretations cannot, therefore, be held as inviolable as Allah's words themselves are. I believe that the correct interpretation of some of the complex terms, like *Riba*, can be found in the Qur'aan itself. The interpretation which is incompatible with the Qur'aanic interpretation should be rejected. This booklet is my humble attempt to depict the Qur'aanic interpretation of *Riba*. Readers should, however, check the contents of

ISLAM & INTEREST

this booklet with their own study of the Qur'aan to satisfy their consciences that whatever stated therein (the booklet) is the truth. They should do this with every book on Islam that they care to read. It is a duty unto them; for, at stake is their perpetually happy and carefree existence in the Hereafter. The alternative, there, is, Allah forbid, perpetual suffering.

Muhammad Shafi
Mumbai, India
24th June 1998

PREFACE TO THE SECOND EDITION

In this edition, I have corrected the minor errors that had crept in, in the first. I have besides added a paragraph to Chapter 4, and 3 Appendices, I II III, at the end of the booklet. I have also effected a change in the title to make it more appropriate and comprehensible. I hope

ISLAM & INTEREST

these additions and changes will lend strength to the point of view depicted in the booklet.

Muhammad Shafi
Mumbai, India
22nd January 2000

PREFACE TO THE THIRD EDITION

I have now thoroughly revised the six Chapters of the earlier Edition and added five more. The main book is now an integrated whole, unlike the earlier Editions wherein the Chapters had been written for their independent publications, individually. There had been criticism from some quarters that the *ahaadeeth* (Traditions) on the subject matter had almost completely been ignored in the earlier Editions. To meet this criticism, four of the five new Chapters added in this Edition deal exclusively with the relevant *ahaadeeth*. A fourth Appendix has also been added in this context. The three Appendices of the earlier Edition have been

ISLAM & INTEREST

retained as they were. Readers may therefore find some points, already made in the Chapters of the main book, repeated in these Appendices. The repetitions may however usefully serve as differently presented reminders of those points. The last of the five Chapters added deals with the questions of Insurance and copyright in so far as they are related to the theme, *Ar-Riba*, of the book. I have again made a change in the title of the book to bring it in tune with the Qur'aanic expression. A subtitle has been added to highlight the fact that the divine commandments discussed in the book are also the divinely ordained Principles of Economics. One other distinguishing feature of this electronic Edition is the Links provided within the book. This would enable the readers to get instant accesses to sections where specific terms/words are more elaborately dealt with.

I pray Allah Almighty to make this revised Edition of the book more effectively serve as a tool to bring the Muslims – and more generally,

ISLAM & INTEREST

mankind – back to the pure Qur'aanic teachings and thus to His Right Path. Amen!

Mohammad Shafi
Mumbai, INDIA
13th December 2000.

PREFACE TO THE FOURTH EDITION

This edition is for print. And I have changed the title to make it indicate the subject matter of the book better, to people in general. No other changes are made.

Mohammad Shafi
Mumbai, INDIA
29th July 2007

ISLAM & INTEREST

PREFACE TO THE FIFTH EDITION

The book has been revised to remove errors in the previous editions.

Mohammad Shafi
Mumbai, INDIA
25th October 2010

ISLAM & INTEREST

CHAPTER 1
WHAT IS *AR-RIBA*?

1.1 In the 39th verse of the 30th Chapter of the Qur'aan [Q: 30.39], it is stated, "And when you give out anything for profit (*minriban*) in a way that the gain is effected by taking the rightful properties, earnings or dues of others (*fee amwaalinnasi*), then that is not a gain at all (*fala yarbu*) with Allah. And the real gainers are those who give out in charity (*min zakatin*), thereby seeking Allah's pleasure."

1.1.1 The verse was the first in the Qur'aan, in order of its revelation, to discuss the subject of *Ar-Riba*. *Riba* or *Riban*, in Arabic, literally means 'gain', 'increase' or 'growth'. Its verb form is *rubuww*, which in turn means 'to increase' or 'to grow'.

1.1.2 Obviously, it is not every gain, profit or increase that is despised by Allah in this verse. It is only a particular kind of it that is despised – the kind that is effected *fee amwaalinnasi* (i.e. in people's amwaal).

Chapter 1

1.1.3 People's *amwaal* are their own rightful possessions. The term includes their rightful earnings, which they have not yet come in possession of: the salary rightfully earned by an employee, for example, which the employer has not yet paid. The term also includes other rightful dues, as for instance, anything given by one person from his own rightful possessions to another for temporary use of it by the latter or for safe custody.

1.1.4 It is thus clear, from the first part of the verse, that what Allah disapproves of is one kind of gain, and not all gains. That particular kind is the one that is effected by taking the *amwaal* – not one's own but – of others. Allah abhors such gains obviously because of the injustice involved in those. The gainers in such cases do, as a matter of fact, usurp what should rightfully belong to others.

1.1.5 The kind of *Riba* (gain) that Allah abhors is further explained in the same verse by

Chapter 1

contrasting it with *Zakat* (charity). When you give something in *Zakat*, you give something of your own *amwaal* to others without expecting anything in return from the recipients. In the said kind of *Riba*, on the other hand, you would be usurping something of others' *amwaal*, in addition to getting your own back.

1.1.6 In this verse, thus, Allah unequivocally defines the kind of *Riba* that He abhors. It is the gain that any party to a transaction contrives or manipulates to get by usurping the rightful dues, earnings or possessions of others. In verses subsequently revealed on the subject matter, this kind of *Riba* has been referred to as *Ar-Riba*. In this term, *Riba* is prefixed with the Arabic definite article *Al*, which is equivalent to the English 'the', but the term is pronounced as *Ar-Riba*. The *Al* prefixed to *Riba* in all the subsequently revealed verses unmistakably indicates the kind of *Riba* described in this verse, viz., Q: 30.39.

Chapter 1

1.1.7 Contrary to the general belief, therefore, *Ar-Riba* stands very well defined in the Qur'aan. Not only is it well defined, but is further variously explained in other verses, as we shall presently see, to make us understand the term properly. It is to be noted that in verse, Q: 30.39, *Ar-Riba* has been described and condemned but not prohibited.

1.2 In accordance with a rule followed in the Qur'aan in taking gradual steps for eradication of an evil practice, *Ar-Riba*, condemned in the verse quoted above, was subjected to restrictions in the next verse revealed thereon. The next verse, viz. Q: 3.130, states: "O believers, do not devour *Ar-Riba* at doubled and redoubled rates. And be conscious of Allah for your own good."

1.2.1 As may be seen, taking of exorbitant *Ar-Riba* was prohibited in this verse, but it was still not a total prohibition. It was so done perhaps not to create a sudden void in the general

Chapter 1

economy of that time. Instead, stress was laid on piety and self-restraint.

1.2.2 What is to be noted, however, is that the kind of *Riba* that was defined in the earlier verse, Q: 30.39, came to be referred to as *Ar-Riba* from this verse [Q: 3.130].

1.3 The next verse revealed on the subject matter is Q: 4.161. It states, "And they took *Ar-Riba* though they were forbidden to do so and devoured people's *amwaal* wrongfully. And We have prepared a painful suffering for those who cover the Truth (i.e. who are nonbelievers) among them."

1.3.1 The pronoun 'they' in this verse stands for the Jews. *Ar-Riba* had been prohibited to them. Allah informs Muslims about this to prepare them for the prohibition that would soon be coming on them (the Muslims) too.

Chapter 1

1.3.2 The Muslims are thus warned of the consequences of disobeying the injunction.

1.3.3 They are also hereby given a further explanation or elaboration of the Qur'aanic meaning of *Ar-Riba*. They are informed that the term applies to wrongful acquisition (usurpation) of other people's *amwaal*.

1.4 We now come to the group of verses with which Allah completed His instructions on *Ar-Riba*. These verses were among the last ones of the Qur'aan in order of its revelation.

1.5 The first verse in the said group is Q: 2.275. It states, "Those who devour *Ar-Riba* do not stand but as one on whom the Satan has cast his spell by touch. This is so because they insist that business (*bai'a*) is like *Ar-Riba*. And Allah has permitted business and prohibited *Ar-Riba*. So then, one, who desists, after receiving admonition from one's Lord, shall retain one's past gains and that one's case shall be left to

Chapter 1

Allah for decision. And the ones who persist shall be those who would inhabit the Fire, therein to abide."

1.5.1 It is in this verse of the Qur'aan that Allah finally and totally prohibits *Ar-Riba*. At the same time, He declares *bai'a*, i.e. business (wherein commodities or services are traded for reasonable profit), to be a permitted activity.

1.5.2 A very significant feature of this verse is that it has pointedly referred to the misinterpretation that the term, *Ar-Riba*, is subjected to at the hands of some people. These people do so under satanic influence. Under this deceitful influence, they liken business to *Ar-Riba*.

1.5.3 I have no knowledge of such people so misinterpreting *Ar-Riba* at the time the Qur'aan was revealed. But I am aware of such people in my age. They condemn one of such businesses, which Allah has permitted, as *Ar-Riba*. They do

Chapter 1

not mind, however, themselves devouring other people's *amwaal*!

1.5.4 They do so in various subtle ways. Some evade taxes due to Government and other statutory institutions. Some, engaged as traders, take advantage of a situation of scarcity to enhance their profit margins substantially. Employers underpay their employees. Employees shirk their work but receive their full salaries. Taxi-drivers demand money, more than the metre-readings, on some pretext or the other.

1.5.5 Such ways are a legend and can be found in every field of activity. Among the perpetrators, unfortunately, are even some who are very religious. They have a holier-than-thou attitude but are blissfully unaware that they are themselves guilty of taking *Ar-Riba*.

1.5.6 And such are the people described as being under the satanic spell in the verse.

Chapter 1

1.5.7 Allah then declares in the verse a general amnesty to those who desist from *Ar-Riba*. Although such people retain their gains due to past *Ar-Riba* dealings, their fates in the Hereafter are left to Allah's decision. The decision perhaps would depend on their future behaviour.

1.5.8 But as for those who persist in *Ar-Riba*, their fates in the Hereafter are sealed. They will go to Hell.

1.6 The next verse, Q: 2.276, declares, "Allah annihilates *Ar-Riba* and renders fulfilling of obligations to the poor and needy, fruitful. And Allah loves not any sinful suppressors of Truth (non-believers)."

1.6.1 This verse gives further expression to Allah's utter displeasure against perpetrators of *Ar-Riba*. At the micro level, the displeasure may not immediately be discernible in cases of

Chapter 1

individuals. A person indulging in *Ar-Riba* may continue for some time to appear prosperous. Allah gives him/her a long rope. The person may even be seen departing from this world still apparently prosperous. Allah's warning is basically for the other world. Life in this world is after all infinitesimally small compared to the interminable life in the other. Still, Allah makes examples of some such persons in this very world and annihilates their ill-gotten wealth. For others to take heed.

1.6.2 At the macro level of communities or nations, however, Allah's displeasure at *Ar-Riba* dealings is very much discernible. Nations and communities wherein corruption is rampant have their economies in doldrums. Economic corruption is nothing but *Ar-Riba*. No nation is free from corruption. But nations, which are less prone to this malady, are the ones that have better economies even when such nations may not be endowed much with natural resources.

Chapter 1

1.6.3 *Ar-Riba* has been contrasted in this verse with *Sadaqaat*. The latter Arabic term is used for payment of moral dues to the deserving, including the poor and needy. The Qur'aan says elsewhere, [Q: 9.60], that Allah has made *Sadaqaat* obligatory. This indicates that *Ar-Riba* dealings involve non-fulfilment of moral obligations in human transactions. A little reflection will show that Allah has here elaborated the meaning of *Ar-Riba*, which had already been defined previously in verse Q: 30.39.

1.7 Now we come to the last two (in order of revelation) verses specifically regarding *Ar-Riba*. These are taken together here, as these are closely inter-linked: "O believers! Fear Allah and give up what remains of *Ar-Riba*, if you do really believe. And if you do not do so (i.e. give up *Ar-Riba*), then be warned that you are in a state of war with Allah and His Messenger. And if you repent, then you are entitled to get back

Chapter 1

your capital dues. You shall wrong not, nor shall you be wronged." [Q: 2.278 & 279]

1.7.1 These verses too are very important in understanding the Qur'aanic concept of *Ar-Riba*. In the first of these two verses, Allah Almighty once again stresses the enormity of the crime of *Ar-Riba*. It is a crime against humanity. It is the perpetrator of economic injustices and disorders in this world. It is one of the primary causes of all the troubles here. It leads humanity away from the straight path Allah has laid down for it. That is why He declares that those who indulge in *Ar-Riba* are at war with Him and His Messenger.

1.7.2 Then, in the second of the two verses, Allah declares that those who desist from taking *Ar-Riba* have the right to take back their capital dues. The actual Arabic word used for dues is *amwaal*. We have seen what *amwaal* generally means in 1.1.3 above. But one important aspect

Chapter 1

of this word needs to be stressed here in order to understand *Ar-Riba* properly.

1.7.3 And in order to understand this aspect, it should first be clearly understood that money is not *amwaal* per se. Money is only the current value of *amwaal*. *Amwaal* of the same quantity and quality may have different values at different points of time. If one kilogram of sugar of a certain quality costs 16 units of money now, it might have cost only 8 units 10 years ago. If one hour of labour now costs 20 units of money, it might have cost, say, 9 units only, 10 years ago. Thus, while *amwaal* (sugar and labour, in the examples given here) remain the same, their value in terms of money may change.

1.7.4 Now it should carefully be noted that Allah, in His all-encompassing wisdom, has always referred to *Ar-Riba* in terms of *amwaal* and not in terms of their value, i.e. money. In the verses presently under discussion too, He

Chapter 1

tells us that we are entitled to get back our capital *amwaal* (and not sums, as some have erroneously translated the word). Let us consider, more elaborately, what this means.

1.7.5 Suppose I am quite rich (although, in fact, I am not). And I have a friend, who is also quite rich. But, two years back, my friend was in financial difficulties and then he needed a car very badly. I had then just bought a car of X brand and Y model. I gave it to the friend and bought another for me. Now, two years after that event, my friend has got over his financial difficulties and wants to pay back the loan.

1.7.6 How can he do that? He cannot just hand over to me the car he has been using for two years. If he does that, I am wronged, and Allah says, in the verse under discussion, that I should not be wronged. I would not be wronged in this case only if I now need another car and my friend gives me a brand-new car of the same X brand and Y model. That too if, as a friendly

Chapter 1

gesture, I do not ask for any compensation from my friend, for his two-year use of my car.

1.7.7 But what if I do not want now to have that type of car and want to have the costlier Z model? I cannot ask my friend to give me the Z model; for, if I do so my friend would be wronged, and I would (Allah forbid) be going against Allah's express command in the verse under discussion. Therefore, the only right course for my friend to adopt would be to give me the present market price of a new car of the X brand and Y model. He should do so even if the price of the said car had appreciated by a few thousand units of money during the two-year period. Then only would neither party be wronged.

1.7.8 On the same analogy, had my friend taken from me the cost, say a quarter million units of money, of the car then and not the car itself, he should pay me now the quarter million plus the few thousands by which the price has

Chapter 1

appreciated. And had my friend taken the money, not for buying a car, but for meeting some urgent domestic need of his, he has now to pay me the present equivalent of the amount calculated as per the consumer price index. If the index has increased by 10%, the amount to be returned by my friend has also to be increased by the same percentage.

1.7.9 Money, as a matter of fact, is not a material thing. It is a power – a power to purchase material things or services. When I gave my friend the said amount two years back, I gave him a certain purchasing power. That purchasing power, and not the amount as such, constituted the *amwaal* of Qur'aanic terminology in this case. My friend must return that principal *amwaal* i.e. that principal purchasing power. If he returns to me only the same amount he would be returning less than my principal *amwaal*. I would be wronged then, and the divine commandment would be vitiated.

Chapter 1

1.7.10 And had my friend taken the money for investment in a new commercial venture of his, the parameter for the return of the loan would change. He would have now to pay me not only the present value of the purchasing power he had taken from me, but also in addition the proportionate share in the profit the venture might have earned during the period. It would be wrong and unjust on the part of my friend if he does not give me this share; for, without the loan I had given him, the commercial venture could not have been brought to fruition. Profits are the *amwaal* earned in the venture. These profits were the result brought about by three factors:
    a. Capital invested by my friend himself,
    b. Loan I had given, and,
    c. Services put in by my friend.

Every one of these three factors shall have a rightful proportionate share in the profits. The three shares of the three factors are therefore their respective rightfully earned *amwaal*. If my friend does not give me the share due to factor

Chapter 1

b, it would be tantamount to his seeking increase in his wealth by usurping my *amwaal* – a clear case of *Ar-Riba* in terms of verse Q: 30.39.

1.7.11 It may be noted here that when I gave the loan to my friend, I provided him with a thing he needed. It was just like the grocer providing groceries for my family's needs or a builder constructing office premises for me for running my business. Both the grocer and the builder take from me their service charges in addition to the costs to them of the things they give me. That is the general basis on which all human transactions are done. Such service charges are never subject to the use or misuse, productive or unproductive, to which the things supplied are put to by the recipients. As for example, the builder does not base his service charges on the success or failure of the business I conduct through the office he built for me. Neither would the grocer repay me his profit margin on the eggs that I bought from him but broke,

Chapter 1

falling accidentally down from my hand on my way home.

1.7.12 Such service charges or profits, or whatever you call them, are worked out, as a norm, at predetermined fixed rates. Nothing wrong in this from the Islamic point of view. Reasonable service charges are the rightful *amwaal* of the service providers, and these must necessarily be at fixed rates depending on the efforts put in and time consumed in providing the services. These charges are also subject, of course, to the open market forces.

1.7.13 There is no reason therefore why I should have necessarily subjected the returns on my loan, given to my friend two years back, on the success or failure of his venture. Unless, of course, we had both agreed to be partners in the venture. Since we had not, I had the right to claim compensation for the deprival to me for two years of the equivalent purchasing power then. I could have utilised the loan amount for

Chapter 1

purchasing things for my own business and earned profits thereon during that period. I could therefore justifiably claim the compensation at a reasonable pre-determined fixed rate (say, the rate at which I earned my profits on my investments two years back), just as the grocer and the builder do in claiming their service charges or profits.

1.7.14 That Islam (as propounded basically in the Qur'aan) does not permit recovery of service charge or any compensation (even if it be called as interest) at fixed rates, is a myth. What Islam requires is that such rates should be justifiable and reasonable and determined on the principle that neither the service provider nor the service recipient should be wronged. It is another matter that in the present example, I may not ask for any compensation out of consideration for a friend, but I do have the right.

Chapter 1

1.8 The Qur'aan does not deny anyone his/her due rights. But it strongly advises all human beings to be humane too while claiming their due rights. Let us now consider this divine advice as a fitting finale to this Chapter discussing the Qur'aanic verses on *Ar-Riba*.

1.8.1 In verse Q: 2.280, which immediately follows the *Ar-Riba* verses mentioned above, Allah says, "And if he (the recipient of services) be in difficulties, then grant him time till it is easy for him to discharge his liabilities. And if you remit your dues in deserving cases, it would be for your good, if you but knew."

1.8.2 Remittance of one's dues in deserving cases is termed as *Sadaqah* or one's moral obligation in the verse. To understand the obligation, let me extend the case, mentioned herein above, of my giving a loan to my friend. If I find that the friend continues to be in financial difficulties, I have to grant him further necessary extensions for making the repayment.

Chapter 1

And, suppose, my financial condition continues to be rosy, while his deteriorates to the extent that he would not be able to repay the loan in the foreseeable future. Then, in view of this Qur'aanic verse, it would be my moral obligation to remit the loan. As a true Muslim, I should have the innate faith in me that Almighty Allah shall make this *Sadaqah* fruitful for me as promised by Him in verse Q: 2.276.

1.9 I believe that a dispassionate, unprejudiced, sincere and meticulous study of the verses quoted above shall reveal to an ardent student of the Qur'aan that the divine injunction on *Ar-Riba* is

    a) Aimed at eliminating injustices in all human transactions,
    b) Well-defined and well-explained in the Qur'aan itself,
    c) A commandment, the violation of which is very, very seriously viewed by Allah – to such an

Chapter 1

extent that He has declared a war on the violators and has promised them the Hell,

d) However, grossly misunderstood by equating Ar-Riba to 'interest' as such, and,

e) Therefore, widely violated by Muslims themselves, thus inviting Allah's ire on them, which is very much reflected in the pathetic present-day status and condition of their community, generally, the world over.

ISLAM & INTEREST

CHAPTER 2
ISLAM & BANK INTEREST - I

2.1 Most religious leaders in the Islamic world today, declare that interest, given and taken by banks, is prohibited in Islam. They even go to the extent of saying that the salaries drawn by bank employees are unlawful earnings. Such leaders are of the opinion that bank interest is covered by the prohibition on *Ar-Riba*, ordered by Allah in verse [Q: 2.275].

2.2 The question is whether bank interest really is *Ar-Riba*, as the religious leaders vehemently assert. No banks, as we find them today, were operating at the time of the Prophet [*sallalLahu alayhi wa sallam* (may Allah's blessings and peace be upon him)]. And, the verse quoted above, was one of the last verses revealed to the Prophet, who passed away soon afterwards. In the circumstances, we do not have the advantage of a *hadheeth* (Tradition) of the Prophet himself explaining in detail the significance and implication of the prohibition on *Ar-Riba*.

Chapter 2

2.3 We do, nevertheless, have the advantage of six more Qur'aanic verses, besides the one quoted above, exclusively dealing with the subject of *Ar-Riba*. We must turn to these verses for guidance.

2.4 Let us take the specific and the most common case of a person, say A, keeping his money in a Savings Account of a bank. He keeps it there, not for earning more money thereon, but for safe custody. At the end of the year, the bank, on its own, adds a small amount to the balance in A's account as interest calculated at the rate, say, of 5%. Noticing that a sizable amount has accumulated in A's account, the bank Manager advises him to keep part of the money as a term deposit, so that A could get more interest, say, at 10%, and A obliges. Is the 5%, or even the 10%, interest taken by A, *Ar-Riba*? And is he therefore guilty of violating the Qur'aanic injunction, quoted above?

Chapter 2

2.5 Let us assume that an amount of Rs. 1000/- was lying in A's account for a year, at the end of which the amount gets increased to Rs. 1050/- because of the addition of interest. Another amount of Rs. 1000/-, kept as a term deposit by A, similarly gets increased to Rs. 1100/-. A, however, finds that, because of the general inflation, what goods he could buy with Rs. 2000/- a year ago, can only be bought with Rs. 2300/-, now! In other words, he finds that the bank is giving him less than the real worth of the Rs. 2000/- he had kept with it a year back. In terms of the real value of the deposits he made a year ago, he is not getting even his principal amount back, let alone getting any addition thereto.

2.6 We may now examine A's situation in the light of the Qur'aanic verses on *Ar-Riba*. We find that in verse Q: 2.279, after giving a stern warning to *Ar-Riba*-takers, Allah says

Chapter 2

that those who forsake taking *Ar-Riba*, are entitled to get back their own *amwaal*, i.e. what is due to them, so that neither do they wrong others, nor are themselves wronged. Under Divine law, therefore, A, himself, is wronged when the bank gives him Rs. 2150/-
He would have been wronged more, had the bank given him Rs. 2000/- only.

2.7 Therefore, in the circumstances mentioned, A is not at all guilty of taking Ar-Riba, when he accepts Rs. 2150/- from the bank. Those who would call him a sinner therefor, are themselves guilty of putting a false allegation on him, that too, in the name of Allah!

2.8 In the example given above, would A have got back his full due, as permitted in the Qur'aanic law, had the bank given him Rs. 2300/-? Let us examine this question now.

2.9 As everyone knows, the amount of Rs. 2000/- deposited by A in the bank, was not kept

Chapter 2

idly lying there. It might have been lent out to someone for being invested in some business or industry. Banks give loans on interests at fixed rates.

2.10 Whether taking of such interests amounts to *Ar-Riba*, will have to be dealt with separately for the sake of clarity in understanding things properly. (The question is dealt with in the next Chapter.) Further, it must be clarified here that working out of profit that a bank makes in a particular year is a complicated affair which has to take into account many factors like bad debts, delayed returns, expenses etc. A good bank lends money very cautiously, taking care that the borrower is reliable and capable of returning all the dues of the bank in good time. As such, on an average, it makes a good profit. Otherwise it cannot survive.

2.11 Now let us suppose that A's bank makes a net profit, say, of 3%. Again, for the sake of clear understanding of the answer to the

Chapter 2

question posed above, let us assume that the bank is making this profit by investing the entire funds, at its disposal, in its own business. Now this profit is not made entirely because of the services put in by the bank. Some credit for the profit also must go to the capital made up of the account holders' money. Without this capital there would be no profit. So, the principles of natural justice demand that in order to give A, his full dues, he should be given an appropriate dividend in addition to Rs. 2300/-. Does Qur'aanic law confirm this conclusion?

2.12 We have seen in Chapter 1 that in terms of verse Q: 30.39, *Ar-Riba* is usurpation of what are other people's *amwaal* [i.e. possessions, earnings or dues] for the dubious satisfaction of seeing one's own worldly wealth increase. Now in the example under study, commonsense tells us that A should have a share in the profit made by the bank. That share is A's rightful due, which the bank is not giving to him. In other words, the bank is usurping A's

Chapter 2

dues. The bank is therefore guilty of taking *Ar-Riba* at A's cost. And in terms of verse Q: 2.279 quoted above, A is the '*mazloom*', or the wronged one, in this case. This wrong can be undone only by the bank giving the due dividend to A.

2.13 So, in the Qur'aanic scheme of things, A should receive from the bank, not only Rs. 2300/- as the full present value of the deposit he made a year ago, but also, in addition, a dividend on the profit made by the bank during the year.

ISLAM & INTEREST

CHAPTER 3
ISLAM & BANK INTEREST - II

3.1 In the light of the clear-cut Qur'aanic definition of *Ar-Riba* explained in Chapter 1, let us now examine whether the interest, taken at some fixed rate by the banks, is *Ar-Riba*. In other words, we must see whether by taking the interest, the banks are usurping the rightful earnings or dues of others. While examining this question, we should remember the simple logic that one would usurp the rightful dues of others when one grabs things beyond one's own rightful dues.

3.2 Banks lend money generally for business. Suppose A obtains a loan of a million rupees from a bank and invests the same in a business. He makes a profit. Now this profit is due not only to the services rendered by A in the business, but also due to the money that he got from the bank. Without the money, there would be no business and no profit. Logically speaking, therefore, the bank is entitled to a reasonable share of the profit. If the interest rate

Chapter 3

were within this reasonable share, there would be no objection from any quarter.

3.3 But what if (i) the bank interest would mop up almost the entire profit, or, (ii) the profit is less than the bank interest, or, (iii) there is no profit at all. It is the possibility of such adverse eventualities occurring, that has prompted the religious leaders to brand bank interest as *Ar-Riba*. But does such branding conform to the Qur'aanic definition of *Ar-Riba*?

3.4 In order to understand the answer to the question properly, we have first to remind ourselves of the basics of the working of a bank. Banks are in the business of providing money for other businesses, big and small, industrial and commercial. Banking business is an essential business; for, without it, most of the other businesses would come to a grinding halt.

3.5 The banks themselves get the money from the savings accounts kept, and term deposits

Chapter 3

made, by the people with them. To attract these accounts and deposits, the banks have to offer interest thereon. In developing countries like India and Pakistan, the interest rates, it has been observed, are lower than the inflation rates there. Banks are large organizations and they incur large organizational expenses like staff salaries, building rentals etc.

3.6 The banks have therefore legitimately to charge interest at rates enough to cover all their expenses and make a reasonable profit. The profit margin must be as small as possible; for, otherwise, the prospective borrowers would go to other banks where the lending rates are lower. In this scenario, no one can, by any stretch of imagination, say that what the banks are getting, by way of interest, are not their rightful earnings or dues. The banks cannot therefore be justifiably accused of usurping the rightful dues or earnings of others. They cannot, in other words, be accused of taking *Ar-Riba*, in terms of the Qur'aan.

Chapter 3

3.7 The banks cannot therefore be accused of taking *Ar-Riba* even in the extreme case of the borrower sustaining a loss in his business. The banks cannot be held responsible for the loss. The responsibility for and the risk of investing the money in the borrower's business are entirely that of the borrower. The bank is concerned with its own business - the banking business. Like any other business, it has a right to claim a reasonable profit for the service it is rendering, viz., of providing the money for other businesses. The money lent plus proportionate expenses incurred plus a reasonable profit, are the legitimate dues of the bank payable by the borrower. These legitimate dues cannot be denied to the Bank even when the borrower sustains a loss in his business. This is just as a seller of steel cannot be legally denied his dues from a builder who had purchased the steel on credit, but the building which he was constructing had collapsed, for reasons which had nothing to do with steel.

Chapter 3

3.8 The argument in the foregoing paragraph derives additional support from the Qur'aanic verse 2.279 stating that a person, desisting from taking *Ar-Riba*, is entitled to his *amwaal*, i.e. to his rightful earnings and dues. This verse makes it crystal clear that claiming of one's rightful earnings or dues, is not *Ar-Riba* even when the borrower sustains a loss. The Qur'aan, however, advises the lender (i.e. the bank here) to give more time to the borrower, in such cases, to enable the latter to return the dues of the former. In the extreme case of the borrower going bankrupt the Qur'aan advices that it would be better for the lender to write-off his dues [Q: 2.280]. A good, reputed bank would do just that. It would provide for such write-offs.

3.9 From the detailed discussions above in this Chapter and in paragraphs 1.7.11 to 1.7.14 of Chapter 1, it should be abundantly clear that bank interest, as generally obtaining in the

Chapter 3

present-day world, is not *Ar-Riba*, in terms of its Qur'aanic definition. That Islam bans such interest as being *Ar-Riba*, is a fallacy. The tragedy is that the fallacy is perpetrated and perpetuated by the protagonists of the religion themselves!

ISLAM & INTEREST

CHAPTER 4
A MODEL ISLAMIC BANK

4.1 We know that banking business is an essential business in the modern-day world. This business provides the other businesses with money, without which no business can be run. Muslims, being part of this world, have, of necessity, to deal with this business of banking. They cannot just wish it away.

4.2 There has got to be then a situation where in a Muslim organization, professing to be conducting its affairs strictly on the Qur'aanic law, is called upon to run a bank. How would it do it?

4.3 Such an organization would, first, scrupulously examine whether this essential business of banking is in any way unlawful under the Qur'aanic law. This business basically comprises collection of money for providing the same to other businesses. Commonsense, or a natural law, would not find anything immoral or unlawful in this business as such. Qur'aanic law is a natural law and there is no specific

Chapter 4

prohibition therein to conducting such a business provided the other businesses, to which money is supplied, are not unlawful under Islam (e.g. manufacturing alcoholic drinks).

4.4 A business is for sale or exchange of a commodity or service for adequate remuneration. In the banking business, it is a service - that of collecting and supplying money for other businesses - that is sold or exchanged for an adequate remuneration. Such sale or exchange (*bai'a* in Arabic) has been specifically ordained as lawful activity in the Qur'aan, while prohibiting *Ar-Riba,* vide verse Q: 2.275. *Ar-Riba,* as we have seen in the preceding Chapters, is iniquitous usurpation of other people's rightful dues or earnings.

4.5 So, a truly Islamic organization would have no objection to itself running a bank, provided, it fulfils the following two conditions.

Chapter 4

a. It binds itself in its Constitution not to lend money for any activity, prohibited in Islam, like manufacturing or selling alcoholic drinks etc., and,
b. It strictly abides by the Qur'aanic injunction on *Ar-Riba*; i.e., it does not, in any way, iniquitously usurp anybody's rightful dues or earnings.

4.6 The Islamic organization has then to lay down its policy on collection of money from its account holders and depositors. This policy would have to adhere to condition (b) mentioned in the foregoing paragraph. The account holders and the depositors would have to be given their rightful dues. The organization would therefore have carefully to ascertain what those rightful dues would be.

4.7 Suppose a depositor, say A, deposits a sum of a hundred thousand rupees in the Islamic bank, for a year. (Here we are not dealing with the question whether it is Islamic for a Muslim

Chapter 4

to make such a deposit. This question is dealt with in the next Chapter.) If the bank returns the same amount to A at the end of the year, A will be wronged in the circumstances of the present-day world. Because of inflation, A finds that the quantum of goods he can buy now with the said sum is less than the quantum he could buy a year ago, with the same sum. In accordance with Qur'aanic law, A is entitled to the return of his *amwaal*, i.e. his goods or dues [see Q: 2.279], and not merely the money. Money, after all, is a token representing the current value of goods; it is not goods, as such, in the common sense of the word.

4.8 To make the point, made in the foregoing paragraph, clear, let us assume that B gives C a new vehicle, worth a hundred thousand rupees, for the latter's use for a year. As per the Qur'aanic law, C must return to B, at the end of the year, an exactly similar new vehicle, and not the used one. C must buy a new vehicle to give it to B, even if it now costs fifteen thousand

Chapter 4

rupees more. Alternatively, C can give, in cash, Rs.115 thousand to B, to abide by the Qur'aanic law, even when the vehicle was bought by B for Rs. 100 thousand only, a year back. If the amount so exchanged were less than Rs. 115 thousand, B would be wronged, and if it were more, C would be wronged. "You will do no wrong, and neither will you be wronged," the Qur'aan tells the lender [Q: 2.279]. I think this example should make the Islamic law crystal clear.

4.9 So, to return to our example of A making a deposit of a hundred thousand rupees with the Islamic bank for a year, it is as if A has deposited with the bank goods (*amwaal*) whose current value, at the time of the deposit, is a hundred thousand rupees. One year hence, A would be entitled to the same goods - same, both in quality and quantity. And, if the same goods would now cost Rs. 115 thousand, the Islamic bank would have to give Rs. 115 thousand to A. In practical terms, the bank

Chapter 4

would have to ascertain the exact amount that would be equivalent to a 100 thousand rupees of a year ago, by basing the calculation on the average price index of goods. If such amount works out to, say, 113 thousand rupees, the bank would have to give that much amount to A, by way of returning A's original *amwaal* only. We shall examine, later in this Chapter, whether this amount would entirely cover all that is rightfully due to A. The difference, between the amount paid to A at the end of the period of his deposit and the amount he had deposited at the beginning of that period, will have to be put under the expense account head of the bank.

4.10 The Islamic bank, as any other bank does, would make the funds, collected by it, available for other businesses. The collection of funds, the maintenance of numerous accounts and the meticulous examination of the antecedents and reliability of the persons and organizations borrowing the money from the bank, involve

Chapter 4

huge expenses – staff salaries, office building rentals, bad debts etc. These expenses have obviously to be recovered, on pro-rata basis, from the persons and organizations, to whom the funds, collected by the bank, are made available. Besides, the Islamic bank, as any other bank, is entitled to a reasonably adequate net profit of 2 to 3 per cent - a norm accepted in Islam for any lawful business (*bai'a*). The expenses incurred by the bank, together with its reasonable and lawful profit, constitute what is called the interest charged by the bank.

4.11 As we have seen in the discussion above, there is, in such an interest, no element of iniquitous usurpation of any rightful dues and earnings of others. The interest constitutes the rightful dues and earnings of the bank. Such an interest cannot therefore be named, as our religious leaders unfortunately do, as *Ar-Riba* in terms of the Qur'aan. For such leaders, the very word, interest, is taboo; they thoughtlessly and indiscriminately consider it an equivalent of *Ar-*

54

Chapter 4

Riba and thus bring the fair name of Islam to disrepute.

4.12 Now, the reasonable net profit of 2 to 3 per cent, that an Islamic bank would get, is no doubt due to the services it has rendered; but it is also due to the funds deposited with it by its account holders and term-depositors. An Islamic bank would therefore be obliged to give the depositors their dues out of the net profit; otherwise, it will be guilty of usurping the rightful dues of its depositors, i.e., it will be guilty of taking *Ar-Riba*. If the net gain is, say 3%, a fair distribution could be 1% for the depositors and 2% for the bank. The Islamic bank would work out the modalities for a fair distribution of the 1% profit, as a dividend, to its depositors. This dividend will, of course, be exclusive of the depositors' original *amwaal*, which must be returned, at its correct value, as explained herein above.

Chapter 4

4.13 The Islamic bank would be a model employer for its employees. Their salaries would be commensurate with the economic environment in which they are living, so that the lowest-paid employee can get the minimum necessities of life. The bank would always be conscious of the fact that if it fails to give its employees their rightful dues, it would be guilty of indulging in *Ar-Riba*. As has been seen in paragraph 1.6.3 herein above, giving *Sadaqaat* is obligatory on every economically well-placed Muslim. It would be equally obligatory on a corporate body of Muslims, running a successful business. It would therefore be obligatory on the Islamic bank also. Such a bank would necessarily pay the *Sadaqaat* or, earmark the appointed portion of its share of the net profit, for the welfare of Society's poor.

4.14 In order to encourage promising scientists, engineers and other entrepreneurs, the model Islamic Bank should set aside a part of its funds as a Venture Capital Fund. The ventures of such

Chapter 4

entrepreneurs should be financed through this Fund. If the Venture Company thus floated makes profits, the same would be adequately shared by the scientists etc. and the Bank. If, on the other hand, the venture fails, the Bank would bear the entire capital loss, while the entrepreneurs would lose only their time and labour. Such Venture Capital Firms have been known to be very successful in the USA. There is no reason why such venture capital funding should not succeed in other countries provided the funding is done judiciously. The promising entrepreneurs lacking funds would thus be effectively encouraged and the community would get the benefit of their ideas.

ISLAM & INTEREST

CHAPTER 5
AN INDIVIDUAL SANS AR-RIBA

5.1 In the Qur'aan, as we have already seen, taking of *Ar-Riba* has been very severely condemned. The taker of *Ar-Riba* has been warned that he/she would be at war with Allah and His Messenger [see Q: 2.279]. If anyone is a true Muslim, i.e., if he/she sincerely believes in Allah, in His Messenger and in the Hereafter, he/she should take this warning very seriously indeed! He/she should carefully watch out for *Ar-Riba* in his/her day-to-day life and scrupulously avoid it.

5.2 *Ar-Riba*, as indicated in the Qur'aan itself, is the iniquitous usurpation of the rightful dues and earnings of others (see Q: 30.39). A true Muslim has therefore to be careful throughout his adult life that he does not do any thing, as a result of which, the rightful dues and earnings of others get unjustly or illegally usurped by him.

5.3 Generally, persons living below the poverty line are themselves victims of *Ar-Riba*; chances

Chapter 5

of their usurping the rightful dues and earnings of others are less, unless they resort to stealing, robbery or cheating. Stealing and robbery may not be covered by the term, *Ar-Riba*; for, in terms of the Qur'aan, in *Ar-Riba*, something is first given out in order to take back much more than what is rightfully due by usurping the other person's rightful dues (Q: 30.39). In cases of stealing and robbery, nothing is given to the victim. Such crimes are therefore distinct from the crime of *Ar-Riba*, in the Qur'aanic terminology, and are outside the scope of this book.

5.4 But there may be instances of cheating which may come under the broad head of *Ar-Riba*. Suppose, for instance, a door-to-door salesman of small items, sells a new product to a gullible housewife for Rs.200/-, when the same product is available in the open market for Rs.80 only. Here is a clear case of the salesman indulging in *Ar-Riba* (i.e. extracting more money than what is due to him) by means of

Chapter 5

cheating. Or, suppose, a housewife, A, gets some household item, say tea, from her neighbour, B, on loan. A knows that B uses a costly variety of tea having a rich, tasty flavour. But when A returns the loan, she gives B the inferior variety that she herself uses. By so doing, A commits *Ar-Riba*; for, B is entitled to get back the item of the same quality and quantity. There may, or may not, cheating be involved in such transactions, but, nevertheless, *Ar-Riba* these would be.

5.5 Then again there may be a case of a taxi driver demanding more money from his passengers at destination, than what a correct meter would indicate, by manipulating the meter reading or on one pretext or the other. Experienced and hard-hearted passengers may resist the illegal demand and insist on paying the correct fare, but others may not be so strong-willed and may yield to the demand for fear of engaging in a wordy duel with the rough and tough taxi driver and thus creating a scene.

Chapter 5

The taxi driver is, in such cases, extracting more money than what is legally due to him, and is thus guilty of taking *Ar-Riba*.

5.6 In cases of *Ar-Riba*, like the ones mentioned above, there may be a tendency, among the perpetrators of such a crime, to justify the same on their being the have-nots, the poor. "What if we take a little more money from those who have money to burn", they argue. But they are wrong. For one thing, all the victims of such *Ar-Riba*-takers may not have money to burn. Even if some of the victims may have such money, Islam does not permit illegal or immoral means to achieve even undoubtedly good ends, let alone dubious ones. Even when he is beset with difficulties and hardships, a true Muslim should have faith in the ultimate good coming to him, provided he sticks to the righteous path. "Thus, as for him who gives and is conscious of Allah and believes in the truth of the ultimate good - for him shall We make easy the path towards ease," the Qur'aan says (Q: 92.5 to 92.7). An

Chapter 5

individual sans *Ar-Riba*, therefore, would not do any such things, which would amount to taking *Ar-Riba*, even when he is in straitened circumstances.

5.7 Let us now have a look into the life styles, vis-a-vis *Ar-Riba*, of those above the poverty line, including the very rich i.e. those who literally have money to burn. It is such people that Allah exhorts again and again in the Qur'aan to give, `in the path of Allah'. Such giving, in *Zakat*, will bring multiplied recompense to the giver, the Qur'aan promises (Q: 30.39). The multiplied recompense is to be expected from Allah alone. On the other hand, if anything is given in order to get back more than what is due (from the person to whom the thing is given), then, Allah says in the same verse (Q: 30.39), the increase in wealth or possessions, so acquired, is but a mirage really.

5.8 In order to comprehend the full significance of the above-quoted verse, let us consider what

Chapter 5

happens if the Qur'aanic exhortation to give is not abided by. The surplus money, that a man may have, gets spent in buying unnecessary things. He may also get tempted to taste the forbidden fruit and thus acquire unsavoury habits. In course of time, he may get addicted to such habits and his family, to buying sprees. It is like getting addicted to a drug. The family may like to go to Dubai or to Singapore for shopping. To cater to these additional 'needs', the man finds that the surplus money, that he was initially having, has become hopelessly inadequate. He must have more money – lots more – to satiate his insatiably growing desires.

5.9 So what does the man do to get more money? The income tax and the other government taxes, he has been paying, now appear burdensome to him. "Why should I pay to the government from my hard-earned money, when others like me are evading the taxes with impunity?" he argues with himself. "I can make a substantial saving in taxes if I grease the

Chapter 5

palms of the concerned officers with a small amount of money." So, the man illegally usurps to himself what was rightfully due to the government. In the Qur'aanic terminology, he indulges in *Ar-Riba*.

5.10 The man does not stop at that. He just cannot stop. He wants more and more money. He doubles the production in his factory and manages to get more than double the profit by minimising the necessary increase in the expenditure on staff salaries. He does that shrewdly by manipulation of accounts and such other means so that the staff and the workers, in general, are not aware that they are being subtly cheated of their rightful dues. He, nevertheless, thus starts iniquitously usurping the rightful dues of his employees and commits the crime of *Ar-Riba* again.

5.11 This 'commitment' to *Ar-Riba* continues inexorably for the man. He finds that he cannot do without it. He veers round to the view that

Chapter 5

one cannot make 'progress' in this world by being honest and sincere 'and all that bullshit'.

5.12 But, suddenly, after lurking on the sidelines for a long time, nemesis catches up with him. A bolt from the blue hits him badly. A long drawn out legal battle in the courts ends up with his conviction for evasion of government taxes: Heavy penalties and a jail term are imposed on him. The workers in his factory, finding out at long last that they were being cheated of their rightful dues, go on a strike. When calamities come to him, they come in a horde, leaving him a total financial wreck.

5.13 It dawns on him then that the increase in wealth he sought through *Ar-Riba*, is no increase at all, in the long run, but proves to be the cause of the ultimate destruction of even what he had, before he started indulging in *Ar-Riba*. He realises that had he given out in charity the surplus money, which he used in buying unnecessary things for himself and his

Chapter 5

family, he would not have come to such a sorry pass. But, alas, it is too late for him now.

5.14 One may say that the scenario, drawn in the preceding few paragraphs, is too simplistic. In real life, persons (let us hereinafter call them as the transgressors), like the man whose life style is described above, - most of them, at least - do not meet with such a fate, so obviously. That may be true, yes: If the fates of all the transgressors were to be obviously bad - for everyone to see, that is - nobody would dare to be a transgressor. It is the apparent prosperity of the transgressors that spurs others to follow in their footsteps. And therein lies the Divine test, without which, human life in this world would be purposeless.

5.15 But the apparent prosperity does not necessarily mean that the transgressors are a happy lot. Despite their millions, and often because of these millions, they are constantly assailed by one worry or the other. One seeks

Chapter 5

prosperity primarily for being happy. Without happiness, prosperity is meaningless. Besides, Allah does bring at least some of the transgressors to the doom as described herein above in this world itself, to make examples of those who go to the very extreme in their transgressions, for the discerning to take lessons from. If all the transgressors do not meet with that extreme fate, it is because they had not gone to the extreme in their transgressions. But all of them must pay for their transgressions, either here or in the Hereafter.

5.16 So our individual sans *Ar-Riba*, if he is above the poverty line, will not have a life style like those of the transgressors. He will dutifully give the *Sadaqaat/Zakat*, honestly pay all his taxes, scrupulously give all their rightful dues to his employees, and constantly pray to Allah not to let Satan entice him into any other form of *Ar-Riba* or evil. If he still has some surplus, which he does not need immediately but may require in future, he will not just stack this

Chapter 5

surplus away in a strong box at home. He would rather put it in a good bank, preferably in an Islamic bank if there were a branch thereof nearby. He can thereby make his surplus money available for other businesses and at the same time keep it in safe custody till he himself needs it again any time.

5.17 If there were no Islamic bank nearby, he would be confronted with a dilemma. Should he keep the surplus idling away at home, also exposing it thereby to greater safety risks? Or, should he put it in any other good bank, where the funds are made available to morally good businesses as well as to businesses like making and selling wine, which would be immoral in Islam? I think that, in the circumstances, he should choose the latter course. He would, in that case too, be investing in the banking business which is by itself not immoral from the Islamic point of view. The responsibility for the morality of the business, for which the funds are

Chapter 5

taken from the bank, is primarily that of the borrower.

ISLAM & INTEREST

CHAPTER 6
EXAMPLES OF AR-RIBA

6.1 Let us now take an example of *Ar-Riba* from the *ahaadeeth* (Traditions): `Once Bilal brought Barni (a kind of) dates to the Prophet (peace be upon him) and the Prophet asked him, "From where have you brought these?" Bilal replied, "I had some inferior kind of dates and exchanged two *Sa'* (measure) of it for one *Sa'* of Barni dates in order to give it to the Prophet to eat." Thereupon the Prophet said, "Beware! Beware! This is definitely *Ar-Riba*! This is definitely *Ar-Riba*! Do not do so, but if you want to buy (a superior kind of dates) sell the inferior kind of dates for money and then, buy the superior kind of dates with that money.' [Sahih-Al-Bukhari, Vol.3, *Hadeeth* # 506]

6.1.1 Such term-defining examples of *Ar-Riba* are to be rarely found in the *ahaadeeth*. So let us analyse the above example very carefully in order to understand the Qur'aanic meaning of *Ar-Riba*. Bilal (may Allah be pleased with him) had exchanged two measures of the inferior quality of dates for only one measure of the

Chapter 6

superior quality, obviously with a desire to be just, in his own (Bilal's) consideration, to the other person with whom the dates were exchanged. And yet, the Prophet said, it was *Ar-Riba*! Why?

6.1.2 The reason is implicit in the last sentence of the *hadeeth*. The real worth of each of the two kinds of dates could be gauged by their market value in terms of money. Maybe, at the time in question, the market price of the inferior variety was less than half the price of the superior variety. In that case, Bilal would have got more than what he rightfully deserved. The excess that Bilal would thus get would be an iniquitous usurpation of the rightful dues of the other man with whom the dates were exchanged. Vice versa, the other man would get the undue excess. In either case, there would be iniquitous usurpation of the rightful dues of the other person, and hence the transaction would amount to *Ar-Riba*, in terms of the Qur'aanic verse [Q: 30.39]. There could of course have

Chapter 6

been a third possibility - that the market price of the inferior variety was exactly half that of the superior variety. In this third case, obviously, there would be no *Ar-Riba*, but the Prophet would not like the matter to be left to chance or to mere conjecture. He wanted all transactions to be transparently above board. Hence his exclamation, "This is definitely *Ar-Riba*!"

6.1.3 The above-quoted *hadeeth* is an eye-opener for those `Islamic scholars' who dogmatically consider anything (even rightful dues and earnings) taken in the name of interest as *Ar-Riba* and who refuse to see *Ar-Riba* in anything else. That is because the minds of such "scholars" are not truly imbibed with the Qur'aanic concept of *Ar-Riba* as enunciated in the above-quoted and other Qur'aanic verses on *Ar-Riba*.

6.2 Slavery is nominally abolished; but we still hear of bonded labour. This is nothing but economic exploitation of the poor, particularly

Chapter 6

in the villages. Generally, it so happens that the moneyed landlords there, on some occasion or the other, like a daughter's marriage in a poor family, extend monetary loans on mortgage. The poor family is not able to return the loan and its property is forfeited. The family is now completely dependent on the landlord who now employs the entire family to work day long on their own field that has now become his. He gives them a pittance, which just enables them to live on. The situation, with some variations here and there, has been depicted umpteen numbers of times in Hindi films. Such stories are not the products of just the fertile imagination of the celluloid world. The stories are based on reality.

6.2.1 There are two instances of *Ar-Riba* in the story in the foregoing paragraph. In the first instance, although it might have been covered by a duly executed contract, the forfeiture by the landlord of the poor family's land was unjustly usurious. What usually happens is that

Chapter 6

for a paltry sum, say Rs. 5000/-, the land worth much more, say Rs. 50,000/-, is mortgaged. The landlord gives the family a year in which to repay the loan, for which time, interest at an exorbitant rate is charged forcing the family to pay nearly as much interest as the principal amount by the end of the year. The poor family, who could hardly subsist on the income from the land, is unable to pay the amount due, which, along with the interest, has now doubled, and the land gets forfeited to the landlord in terms of the mortgage contract. In such a case, there is a literal manifestation of the definition of *Ar-Riba* given in the above-mentioned Qur'aanic verse Q: 30.39. By lending a small amount of Rs. 5000/-, the landlord sought and obtained an unjustly large increase in his wealth through usurpation of the poor family's land.

6.2.2 In the second instance of *Ar-Riba,* in the story mentioned in paragraph 6.2 above, the landlord extracts work day long from every

Chapter 6

member of the family, including boys and girls who can do some work. The remuneration given to them is barely enough for the family's needs on food and clothing. Earlier, the children did attend the village school, but now the landlord says he cannot afford to provide for the food and clothing of the entire family unless the children also work. So, the children are forced to leave school and start working for the landlord on the field or at his house. If he wanted to, the landlord could have given the family much better wages, for, with better methods and implements of farming which he can well afford, the landlord now gets much better yield from the field than what the poor family could get with their poor resources. The landlord, in other words, is enriching himself at the cost of the poor family by denying them their full wages rightfully due to them and giving them instead only subsistence `allowance', as if out of charity! This is also a clear case of *Ar-Riba* in terms of the Qur'aanic verse quoted above.

Chapter 6

6.2.3 The village story mentioned in paragraph 6.2 above has its urban versions in various forms and with relevant variations. In towns and cities, we see poor people losing their valuables mortgaged for loans, domestic servants and employees of some firms being underpaid and such other cases that too are, nevertheless, examples of *Ar-Riba*.

6.3 In verse Q: 2.275, as we have already seen, the Qur'aan condemns those who say that *bai'a* (business or trading) is like *Ar-Riba* and asserts that Allah has permitted *bai'a* and prohibited *Ar-Riba*. The significance of this Divine statement seems to have been lost on most of our religious leaders. They seem to interpret it to mean that there can be no *Ar-Riba* in any trading activity. We therefore hardly hear any such leader proclaiming an inordinately large profit margin taken in a trading activity, as *Ar-Riba*. But going by the Qur'aanic verse Q: 30.39, taking of such large profit is tantamount

Chapter 6

to *Ar-Riba*. Large profit margins are possible under certain conditions only, such as when one has, or engineers (by hoarding etc.), a monopoly in any trading item. In such conditions, the person who has the monopolistic hold on the item hikes its price to the maximum possible extent, depending on the buying capacity of the general public, to get the maximum possible profit for himself. He thus goes beyond the bounds of his rightful dues in trading the item and seeks to enrich himself by unjustly extracting more money from the ultimate users of the item than what was rightfully due from them. He thus indulges in *Ar-Riba*, although he is engaged in the permitted activity of trading. It may therefore be seen that the Divine statement in verse Q: 2.275, mentioned above, means that what is permitted by Allah is *bai'a* sans *Ar-Riba* i.e. business or trading in which *Ar-Riba* is not indulged in, and that *Ar-Riba* is prohibited in whatever field of activity it is practised.

Chapter 6

6.4 I have been personally conversant with the work 'ethics' of some public servants working in Government offices in India. They were in the habit of coming late to office, took their own time on a wash and a refreshing cup of tea and then, very reluctantly, brought themselves to looking into the long pending files on their table. Soon enough, after they had done with hardly 2 or 3 files of the dozens pending, the lunchtime would arrive. The half-hour lunchtime would be extended to over an hour. If a friend or a relative would not drop in for a chat, some more work on the files would be done. An hour more with the files would be considered more than enough. Rest of the time, till the office closes for the day, would be spent chatting with colleagues or with friends and relatives on the office phone. If there is nothing else personally important, the discussion would veer round, with national pride, to the exploits of our heroes in the last cricket match won by India. Or, if possible and feasible, permission to leave office early would be sought and obtained

Chapter 6

for some urgent and unavoidable domestic errand.

6.4.1 I do not mean to say that all government officials are like those described in the foregoing paragraph, but some are. It is these some, who are the topic of our discussion here. The Government pays them their full salaries for an eight-hour work from them on every working day. It may not be physically possible for a human being, made as he is, to put in an eight-hour work at a stretch, but he can work for, at the least, five of those eight hours honestly and diligently. The officials under discussion do not care to do that; they condescend to work hardly for two to three hours. As a result, they are extracting from the Government more than their rightful dues or earnings. The excess money, they so get is *Ar-Riba*, in terms of the Qur'aanic verse Q: 30.39. The work, such people shun, may have to be attended to by some of their honest colleagues. In that case, the dishonest officials are

Chapter 6

iniquitously usurping the rightful earnings of their honest colleagues, and thus also committing the offence of *Ar-Riba*.

6.5 If one ponders deeply, one would find that *Ar-Riba* lurks, behind the scenes, in almost every walk of life. Any man, who yields to his baser instincts of greed, avarice, lust etc., can easily fall a prey to it. It entices man with quick material prosperity, but once he comes under its snares, he is given the proverbial long rope, which would ultimately lead him to his doom. As Allah warns mankind that if they persist in taking *Ar-Riba*, "then know that you are at war with Allah and His Messenger" [Q: 2.279]: A very ghastly warning indeed for those who believe!

ISLAM & INTEREST

CHAPTER 7
AHAADEETH ON *AR-RIBA* - I

7.1 One *hadeeth* has already been quoted herein above – in paragraph 6.1 – which, on analysis, has been seen to be in conformity with the Qur'aanic concept of *Ar-Riba*. But one critic of the earlier editions of this book says, "Emphasis on Quran with only occasional mentioning of hadith .... is unjustified."

7.2 But before going into an in-depth study of the other *ahaadeeth* on *Ar-Riba*, I would invite my readers to go through some principles on the reliability of *ahaadeeth* enunciated by an Islamic scholar, the Late Allamah Iqbal Ahmad Suhail, in his book *What is Riba*. The principles are extracted in Appendix IV to this book. I find myself in agreement with those principles and the Allamah puts those forth so nicely, that I am wary of restating the same in my own words. It is another matter that I am not in agreement with the Allamah on the definition he has given of *Ar-Riba* (refer my review, in Appendix II, of the Allamah's book).

Chapter 7

7.3 I would also draw my readers' attention, in this context, to one interesting *hadeeth*. It is the one copied below. It is copied from an English translation of Sahih-al-Bukhari. *Volume 7, Book 69, Number 493:*

> Narrated Ibn 'Umar:
> 'Umar delivered a sermon on the pulpit of Allah's Apostle, saying, "Alcoholic drinks were prohibited by Divine Order, and these drinks used to be prepared from five things, i.e., grapes, dates, wheat, barley and honey. Alcoholic drink is that, that disturbs the mind." 'Umar added, "I wish Allah's Apostle had not left us before he had given us definite verdicts concerning three matters, i.e., how much a grandfather may inherit, the inheritance of Al-Kalala, and various types of Riba."

7.4 Let us not allow ourselves to get confused with matters, other than *Ar-Riba*, mentioned in the above *hadeeth*. Let us concentrate on what

Chapter 7

is said therein about *Ar-Riba*. Shorn of the other matters, the *hadeeth* gets reduced to Umar (may Allah be pleased with him) saying, "I wish Allah's Apostle had not left us before he had given us definite verdict concerning various types of Riba."

7.5 Now what does this *hadeeth* mean? Does it mean that Allah's Law concerning *Ar-Riba* was (Allah forbid) imperfect when the Apostle (peace be upon him) left this world? It cannot! For, Allah says, "---This day, I have perfected your religion for you, completed My Favour upon you, and have chosen for you Islam as religion. ---" [Q: 5.3].

7.6 It may thus be seen that a person, with no background knowledge of the Qur'aan, may easily get misled by reading a *hadeeth*. *Ahaadeeth* have therefore got to be studied in the Qur'aanic light.

Chapter 7

7.7 Unfortunately, this illuminating divine light is not used at all by most of the Islamic scholars of today in deciphering the meaning of the prohibited *Ar-Riba*. They seem to think that this Qur'aanic term has not been defined, explained or clarified in the Qur'aan. Such thinking would blasphemously be contrary to the oft-repeated assertion in the Qur'aan that its verses, besides enunciating the divine Law for Mankind, have been amply and elaborately explained and made clear therein (refer verses 3.7, 5.89, 6.46, 6.55, 6.65, 6.98, 6.105, 6.126 and so on).

7.8 To return to the *hadeeth* mentioned in paragraph 7.3 above, why did then such an outstanding personality like Umar say what is attributed to him, regarding *Ar-Riba*? He was one of the most prominent Companions of the Prophet. He was the Ruler of the Muslim world as its 2nd Caliph. During his Caliphate the Muslims reached new heights to become the greatest political and moral force on earth of that time. And history records that he was one

Chapter 7

of the most just, God-fearing and successful personalities that ever ruled on this earth.

7.9 How could such an eminently distinguished Islamic personality make a statement, which, on the face of it, could give the false impression of the Islamic Law on *Ar-Riba* being imperfect?

7.10 Had we pondered deeply over this very significant question, the Muslim Ummah would not have found itself behaving like the proverbial blind men trying to find out what an elephant was like. We have been blind on the question of *Ar-Riba* because of our adamant refusal to go by the illuminating Qur'aanic light in this regard. And, although nobody would confess to it in so many words, we have taken, like those blind men, the partial-truths and half-truths as gleaned and assumed by us from the various individual *Ahaadeeth*, as the whole truth of the real meaning of *Ar-Riba*.

Chapter 7

7.11 As we have already seen herein above, the false impression, which might be created by the *hadeeth* under discussion, is nullified in the light of verse [Q: 5.3]. In this light let us re-examine the statement attributed to the Right Honourable Umar.

7.12 First of all, we should face facts. The facts are that the *ahaadeeth* came to be recorded in writing only generations after the death of the Prophet (peace and blessings of Allah be upon him). Allah bless the *Muhaddiseen* (the compilers in writing of the *ahaadeeth*) of the authentic books of *ahaadeeth* for the excellent, sincere and painstaking work that they had done in ensuring the authenticity of the *ahaadeeth* they had selected for their records. But despite their undoubtedly sincere work, we cannot be cent per cent sure that Umar's statement was exactly in the same words as attributed to him in the *hadeeth* under discussion. We know by hard experience how a statement made by one person gets changed, even unintentionally, by

Chapter 7

the time it is communicated verbally through a chain of, say, half a dozen persons within a span of as little as one hour.

7.13 That is the reason why even authentic *ahaadeeth* need to be checked with relevant Qur'aanic verses, which, on the other hand, got written down immediately after their revelations and got verified and re-verified by none other than the Prophet himself.

7.14 As universally recognised, the sources of any Islamic Law are two, viz., a) the Qur'aan and b) the Sunnah. Umar's statement, read with verse Q: 5.3, should therefore imply that enough clarifications on *Ar-Riba* are not available in the Sunnah. And, since such clarifications are not available in the Sunnah, these oughts to be available in the Qur'aan.

7.15 We can hence conclude that the Qur'aan it is which gives the basic meaning or definition of and clarifications regarding *Ar-Riba*. All the

Chapter 7

ahaadeeth on *Ar-Riba* ought therefore to be understood in the light of this meaning or definition and clarifications. The Muslim Ummah is liable to be led astray otherwise. That is the rational implication of the *hadeeth* quoted herein above in this Chapter.

ISLAM & INTEREST

CHAPTER 8
AHAADEETH ON AR-RIBA – II

8.1 In the preceding Chapter, we have seen why *ahaadeeth* are not as inviolate as Qur'aanic verses are. But this fact should not lead us to any such belief that we can do without the *ahaadeeth*. We cannot. It is through the *ahaadeeth* that we learn the Sunnah, the established practice of our Prophet (Allah's blessings and peace be upon him). And, without Sunnah, certain aspects of Islam, the religion divinely ordained for mankind, would be incomplete. For, Allah says, "---And if you differ on anything amongst yourselves, refer it unto Allah and His Apostle -----" [Q: 4.59].

8.2 The question that may then arise in our minds is as to why Allah Almighty did not make the Sunnah as secure and inviolate as the Qur'aan. In everything that He does there is planning. So, there ought to be some divine purpose in this thing also. Maybe, He is thus testing our steadfast adherence to the undoubtedly inviolate Qur'aan. He is testing us

Chapter 8

whether we examine the *ahaadeeth* blindly, without the illuminating Qur'aanic light.

8.3 Let us therefore pass this divine test by examining the other *ahaadeeth* on *Ar-Riba* also in the light of the relevant Qur'aanic verses, discussed herein above in Chapter 1.

8.4 There are several variants of the *hadeeth* quoted in paragraph 6.1 of Chapter 6. Some of them are reproduced below from the translations of the relevant books of *ahaadeeth*.

(1) Sahih-al-Bukhari, Volume 3, Book 34, Number 294:
Narrated Abu Said:
We used to be given mixed dates and used to sell two Sas of those dates) for one Sa (of good dates). The Prophet said, "No two Sas for one Sa nor two Dirhams for one Dirham is permissible".
(2) Sahih-al-Bukhari, Volume 3, Book 34, Number 405:

Chapter 8

Narrated Abu Said Al-Khudri and Abu Huraira:
Allah's Apostle appointed somebody as a governor of Khaibar. That governor brought to him an excellent kind of dates. The Prophet asked, "Are all the dates of Khaibar like this?" He replied, "By Allah, no, O Allah's Apostle! But we barter one Sa of this (type of dates) for two Sas of dates of ours and two Sas of it for three of ours." Allah's Apostle said, "Do not do so, but sell the mixed dates (of inferior quality) for money, and then buy good dates with that money."

(3) Sahih-al-Bukhari, Volume 3, Book 38, Number 499:
Narrated Abu Said Al-Khudri and Abu Huraira:
Allah's Apostle employed someone as a governor at Khaibar. When the man came to Medina, he brought with him dates called Janib. The Prophet asked

Chapter 8

him, "Are all the dates of Khaibar of this kind?" The man replied, "we exchange two Sa's of bad dates for one Sa of this kind of dates (i.e. Janib), or exchange three Sa's for two." On that, the Prophet said, "Don't do so, as it is a kind of usury (Riba) but sell the dates of inferior quality for money, and then buy Janib with the money". The Prophet said the same thing about dates sold by weight.
(4) Sahih Muslim, Book 010, Number 3869:
Abu Huraira and Abu Sa'id al-Khudri (Allah be pleased with them) reported that Allah's Messenger (may peace be upon him) deputed a person from Banu 'Adi al-Ansari to collect revenue from Khaibar. He came with a fine quality of dates, whereupon Allah's Messenger (may peace be upon him) said to him: Are all the dates of Khaibar like this? He said: Allah's Messenger, it is not so. We buy one sa' of (fine quality of dates)

Chapter 8

for two sa's out of total output (including even the inferior quality of dates), whereupon Allah's Messenger (may peace be upon him) said: Don't do that, but like for like, or sell this (the inferior quality and receive the price) and then buy with the price of that, and that would make up the measure.
(5) Sahih Muslim, Book 010, Number 3870:
Abu Huraira (Allah be pleased with him) reported that Allah's Messenger (may peace be upon him) deputed a person to collect revenue from Khaibar. He brought fine quality of dates, whereupon Allah's Messenger (may peace be upon him) said: Are all the dates of Khaibar like this)? He said: No. We got one sa' (of fine dates) for two sa's (of inferior dates), and two sa's for three sa's. Thereupon Allah's Messenger (may peace be upon him) said: Don't do that rather sell the inferior quality of

Chapter 8

dates for dirhams (money), and then buy the superior quality with the help of dirhams.
(6) Sahih Muslim, Book 010, Number 3871:
Abd Sa'id reported: Bilal (Allah be pleased with him) came with fine quality of dates. Allah's Messenger (may peace be upon him) said to him: From where (you have brought them)? Bilal said: We had inferior quality of dates and I exchanged two sa's (of inferior quality) with one sa (of fine quality) as food for Allah's Apostle (may peace be upon him), whereupon Allah's Messenger (may peace be upon him) said: Woe! it is in fact Riba; therefore, don't do that. But when you intend to buy dates (of superior quality), sell (the inferior quality) in a separate bargain and then buy (the superior quality). And in the hadith transmitted by Ibn Sahl there is no mention of" whereupon".

Chapter 8

(7) Sahih Muslim, Book 010, Number 3872:
Abu Sa'id (Allah be pleased with him) reported: Dates were brought to Allah's Messenger (may peace be upon him), and he said: These dates are not like our dates, whereupon a man said: We sold two sa's of our dates (in order to get) one sa', of these (fine dates), whereupon Allah's Messenger (may peace be upon him) said: That is Riba; so return (these dates of fine quality), and get your (inferior dates) ; then sell our dates (for money) and buy for us (with the help of money) such (fine dates).

(8) Sahih Muslim, Book 010, Number 3873:
Abu Sa'id (Allah be pleased with him) reported: We were given to eat, during the lifetime of Allah's Messenger (may peace be upon him), dates of different qualities mixed together, and we used to sell two sa's of these for one sa, (of fine

Chapter 8

quality of dates). This reached Allah's Messenger (may peace be upon him), whereupon he said: There should be no exchange of two sa's of (inferior) dates for one sa (of fine dates) and two sa's of (inferior) wheat for one sa' of (fine) wheat. and one dirham for two dirharms.
(9) Sahih Muslim, Book 010, Number 3874:
Abu Nadra reported: I asked Ibn Abbas (Allah be pleased with them) about the conversion (of gold and silver for silver and gold). We said: Is it hand to hand exchange? I said: Yes. whereupon he said: There is no harm in it. I informed Abu Sa'id about it, telling him that I had asked Ibn 'Abbas about it and he said: Is it hand to hand exchange? I said: Yes, whereupon he said: There is no harm in it. He (the narrator) said, or he said like it: We will soon write to him, and he will not give you this fatwa (religious verdict). He said: By Allah, someone of

Chapter 8

> the boy-servants of Allah's Messenger (may peace be upon him) brought dates, but he refused to accept them (on the plea) that those did not seem to be of the dates of our land. He said: Something had happened to the dates of our land, or our dates. So, I got these dates (in exchange by giving) excess (of the dates of our land), whereupon he said: You made an addition for getting the fine dates (in exchange) which tantamounts to Riba; don't do that (in future). Whenever you find some doubt (as regards the deteriorating quality of) your dates, sell them, and then buy the dates that you like.

8.5 The *hadeeth* quoted at S. No. (6) in the preceding paragraph is almost the same as the one quoted in paragraph 6.1 herein above. We have already seen in Chapter 6 that this *hadeeth* is in conformity with the Qur'aanic concept of *Ar-Riba* as discussed in Chapter 1.

Chapter 8

8.6 Some students of *ahaadeeth*, however, allege that the definite assertion in this hadeeth that the transaction was tantamount to *Ar-Riba* might have been an interpolation. They say that in the chain of narrators of this *hadeeth*, the later ones might have converted, albeit unintentionally, the conclusion drawn by the earlier ones as the assertion of the Prophet himself. They cite, in support, other *ahaadeeth* like the one at S. No. (1) in paragraph 8.4 above, wherein there is no mention of *Ar-Riba* at all.

8.7 At the time the incidents mentioned in the different *ahaadeeth* (quoted in paragraphs 6.1 and 8.4 above) concerning dates took place, such students allege, the verse prohibiting *Ar-Riba* had not been revealed. The Prophet would not therefore prohibit the exchanges categorically as *Ar-Riba* before Allah had promulgated the prohibition.

Chapter 8

8.8 The argument in the preceding paragraph would also get an indirect support from the *hadeeth* quoted in paragraph 7.3 herein above. Umar would not have expressed his exasperation, as he reportedly did in that *hadeeth*, had there been such clear-cut verdicts from the Prophet on *Ar-Riba* as in the *ahaadeeth* concerning dates.

8.9 And since such students of *ahaadeeth*, unfortunately, did not use the Qur'aanic light, they thought that none of these *ahaadeeth* concerning dates had anything to do with *Ar-Riba*. They thought the Prophet simply wanted people to avoid the injustices that could be involved in those exchanges of inferior dates with superior ones. They were so near to finding the real meaning of *Ar-Riba* in those *ahaadeeth*, and yet did not! Had they used the Qur'aanic light, they would have seen that *Ar-Riba* is nothing but the injustices, potential in all human transactions.

Chapter 8

8.10 Other students of *ahaadeeth*, on the other hand, drew some other conclusions from those *ahaadeeth* concerning dates. Some came to the amazing conclusion that *Ar-Riba* was applicable only to certain commodities! And, 'dates' was one of such commodities since the Prophet had specifically associated *Ar-Riba* with it.

8.11 It is very much obvious from the *ahaadeeth* concerning dates that the Prophet had not permitted exchange of unequal quantities of the same commodity only because of injustices inherent in such exchanges. He therefore had given the people a sort of general rule of 'like for like and hand to hand' in respect of dates, along with some other specified commodities. That is, if any two persons wished to have an exchange in the same commodity, say dates, they should exchange equal quantities thereof on the spot.

8.12 Now it goes without saying that no two sane persons would wish to have such an

Chapter 8

exchange, if both have the same kind or quality of dates. The exchange would be meaningless in that case. So the Prophet could have given the rule only to prevent the possible malpractice of *Ar-Riba* involved in the exchange of different kinds of the same commodity.

8.13 But from this Prophet-given rule, some students of *ahaadeeth* devised another general rule that if one commodity, say dates, is exchanged with another commodity, say wheat, no *Ar-Riba* is involved, whatever the ratio of exchange. This and such other man-made rulings came to be devised out of a lack of understanding of the Qur'aanic meaning of *Ar-Riba*. Had the devisers of this rule been aware that the Qur'aanic meaning of *Ar-Riba* is injustice in any human transaction, they would have seen that there could be *Ar-Riba* in the exchange between different commodities also.

8.14 The Prophet had given his rulings in the specific cases brought, or that came, to his

Chapter 8

notice, as per the divine guidance he was privileged with. It would be wrong for us now to generalise those rulings without the divine guidance still available to us in the Qur'aan.

8.15 In the light of that divine guidance, we can see, as we have already seen in Chapter 6, that the exchanges of different qualities of dates mentioned in all those *ahaadeeth* enumerated in paragraph 8.4 above could amount to *Ar-Riba*. That is why the Prophet (Allah's blessings and peace be upon him) prohibited such exchanges.

ISLAM & INTEREST

CHAPTER 9
AHAADEETH ON *AR-RIBA* – III

9.1 In the preceding Chapter, mention was made of the Prophet-given rule of 'like for like, hand to hand'. Let us here consider some more *ahaadeeth* on this ruling.

9.2 Translations of some such *ahaadeeth* are copied below:

(1) Sahih-al-Bukhari Volume 3, Book 34, Number 379:
Narrated Ibn 'Umar:
The Prophet said, "The selling of wheat for wheat is Riba except if it is handed from hand to hand and equal in amount. Similarly, the selling of barley for barley, is Riba except if it is from hand to hand and equal in amount, and dates for dates is Riba except if it is from hand to hand and equal in amount.

(2) Sahih-al-Bukhari Volume 3, Book 34, Number 382:
Narrated Ibn Shihab:
Malik bin Aus said, "I was in need of change for one-hundred Dinars. Talha

Chapter 9

bin 'Ubaid-Ullah called me and we discussed the matter, and he agreed to change (my Dinars). He took the gold pieces in his hands and fidgeted with them, and then said, "Wait till my storekeeper comes from the forest." 'Umar was listening to that and said, "By Allah! You should not separate from Talha till you get the money from him, for Allah's Apostle said, 'The selling of gold for gold is Riba except if the exchange is from hand to hand and equal in amount, and similarly, the selling of wheat for wheat is Riba unless it is from hand to hand and equal in amount, and the selling of barley for barley is Riba unless it is from hand to hand and equal in amount, and dates for dates, is Riba unless it is from hand to hand and equal in amount"
(3) Sahih Muslim Book 010, Number 3845:

Chapter 9

Abu Salid al-Khudri reported Allah's Messenger (may peace be upon him) as saying: Do not sell gold for gold, except like for like, and don't increase something of it upon something; and don't sell silver unless like for like, and don't increase something of it upon something, and do not sell for ready money something to be given later.
(4) Sahih Muslim Book 010, Number 3846:
Nafi' reported that Ibn 'Umar told him that a person of the tribe of Laith said that Abu Sa'id al-Kludri narrated it (the abovementioned hadith) from tile Messenger of Allah (may peace be upon him) in a narration of Qutaiba. So 'Abduliali and Nafi' went along with him, and in the hadith transmitted by Ibn Rumh (the words are) that Nafi' said: 'Abdullah (b. 'Umar) went and I along with the person belonging to Banu Laith entered (the house) of Sa'id al-Khudri,

Chapter 9

and he ('Abdullah b. Umar) said: I have been informed that you say that Allah's Messenger (may peace be upon him) forbade the sale of silver with silver except in case of like for like, and sale of gold for gold except in case of like for like. Abu Sa'id pointed towards this eyes and his ears with his fingers and said: My eyes saw, and my ears listened to Allah's Messenger (may peace be upon him) saying: Do not sell gold for gold, and do not sell silver for silver except in case of like for like, and do not increase something of it upon something, and do not sell for ready money something, not present, but hand to hand.

(5) Sahih Muslim Book 010, Number 3848:

Abu Sa'id al-Khudri (Allah be pleased with him) reported Allah's Messenger (may peace be upon him) as saying: Do not sell gold for gold and silver for

Chapter 9

silver weight for weight or of the same quality.

(6) Sahih Muslim Book 010, Number 3849:

'Uthman b. 'Affan reported Allah's Messenger (May peace be upon him) as saying: Do not sell a dinar for two dinars and one dirham for two dirhams.

(7) Sahih Muslim Book 010, Number 3850:

Malik b. Aus b. al-Hadathan reported: I came saying who was prepared to exchange dirhams (for my gold), whereupon Talha b. Ubaidullah (Allah be pleased with him) (as he was sitting with 'Umar b. Khattib) said: Show us your gold and then come to us (at a later time). When our servant would come we would give you your silver (dirhams due to you). Thereupon 'Umar b. al-Khattib (Allah be pleased with him) said: Not at all. By Allah, either give him his silver (coins) or return his gold to him, for

Chapter 9

Allah's Messenger (may peace be upon him) said: Exchange of silver for gold (has an element of) Riba in it except when (it is exchanged) on the spot; and wheat for wheat is Riba unless both are handed over on the spot: barley for barley is Riba unless both are handed over on the spot; dates for dates is Riba unless both are handed over on the spot.
(8) Sahih Muslim Book 010, Number 3852:
Abil Qiliba reported: I was in Syria (having) a circle (of friends) in which was Muslim b. Yasir. There came Abu'l-Ash'ath. He (the narrator) said that they (the friends) called him: Abu'l-Ash'ath, Abu'l-Ash'ath, and he sat down. I said to him: Narrate to our brother the hadith of Ubada b. Samit. He said: Yes. We went out on an expedition, Mu'awiya being the leader of the people, and we gained a lot of spoils of war. And there was one silver utensil in what we took as spoils.

Chapter 9

Mu'awiya ordered a person to sell it for payment to the people (soldiers). The people made haste in getting that. The news of (this state of affairs) reached 'Ubada b. Samit, and he stood up and said: I heard Allah's Messenger (may peace be upon him) forbidding the sale of gold by gold, and silver by silver, and wheat by wheat, and barley by barley, and dates by dates, and salt by salt, except like for like and equal for equal. So he who made an addition or who accepted an addition (committed the sin of taking) Riba. So the people returned what they had got. This reached Mu'awiya. and he stood up to deliver an address. He said: What is the matter with people that they narrate from the Messenger (may peace be upon him) such tradition which we did not hear though we saw him (the Holy Prophet) and lived in his company? Thereupon, Ubida b. Samit stood up and repeated

Chapter 9

that narration, and then said: We will definitely narrate what we heard from Allah's Messenger (may peace be upon him) though it may be unpleasant to Mu'awiya (or he said: Even if it is against his will). I do not mind if I do not remain in his troop in the dark night. Hammad said this or something like this.

(9) Sahih Muslim Book 010, Number 3853:

Ubida b. al-Simit (Allah be pleased with him) reported Allah's Messenger (may peace be upon him) as saying: Gold is to be paid for by gold, silver by silver, wheat by wheat, barley by barley, dates by dates, and salt by salt, like for like and equal for equal, payment being made hand to hand. If these classes differ, then sell as you wish if payment is made hand to hand.

(10) Sahih Muslim Book 010, Number 3854:

Chapter 9

Abu Sa'id al-Khudri (Allah be pleased with him) reported Allah's Messenger (may peace be upon him) as saying: Gold is to be paid for by gold, silver by silver, wheat by wheat, barley by barley, dates by dates, salt by salt, like by like, payment being made hand to hand. He who made an addition to it, or asked for an addition, in fact dealt in Riba. The receiver and the giver are equally guilty.
(11) Sahih Muslim Book 010, Number 3856:
Abu Huraira (Allah be pleased with him) reported Allah's Messenger (may peace be upon him) as saying: Dates are to be paid for by dates, wheat by wheat, barley by barley, salt by salt, like for like, payment being made on the spot. He who made an addition or demanded an addition, in fact, dealt in Riba except in case where their classes differ. This hadith has been narrated on the authority of Fudail b. Ghazwan with the same

Chapter 9

chain of transmitters, but he made no mention of (payment being) made on the spot.

(12) Sahih Muslim Book 010, Number 3857:

Abu Huraira (Allah be pleased with him) reported Allah's Messenger (may peace be upon him) as saying: Gold is to be paid for by gold with equal weight, like for like, and silver is to be paid for by silver with equal weight, like for like. He who made an addition to it or demanded an addition dealt in Riba.

(13) Sahih Muslim Book 010, Number 3858:

Abu Huraira (Allah be pleased with him) reported Allah's Messenger (may peace be upon him) as saying: Let dinar be exchanged for dinar, with no addition on either side and dirham be exchanged for dirham with no addition on either side. This hadith has been narrated on

Chapter 9

the authority of Musa b. Abu Tamim with the same chain of transmitters.

(14) Sahih Muslim Book 010, Number 3859:

Abu Minhal reported: My partner sold silver to be paid in the (Hajj) season or (in the days of) Hajj. He (my partner) came to me and informed me, and I said to him: Such transaction is not desirable. He said: I sold it in the market (on loan) but nobody objected to this. I went to al-Bara' b. 'Azib and asked him, and he said: Allah's Apostle (may peace be upon him) came to Medina and we made such transaction, whereupon he said: In case the payment is made on the spot, there is no harm in it, and in case (it is 'sold) on loan, it is Riba. You better go to Zaid b. Arqam, for he is a greater trader than I; so I went to him and asked him, and he said like it.

(15) Sahih Muslim Book 010, Number 3860:

Chapter 9

Habib reported that he heard Abu Minhal as saying: I asked al-Bara' b. Azib about the exchange of (gold for silver or vice versa), whereupon he said: you better ask Zaid b. Arqam for he knows more than I. So I asked Zaid but he said: You better ask al-Bara' for he knows more than I. Then both of them said: Allah's Messenger (may peace be upon him) forbade the sale of silver for gold when payment is to be made in future.

(16) Sahih Muslim Book 010, Number 3861:

Abd al-Rabman b. Abia Bakra reported on the authority of his father that Allah's Messenger (may peace be upon him) forbade the sale of gold for gold, and silver for silver except equal for equal, and commanded us to buy silver for gold as we desired and buy gold for silver as we desired. A person asked him (about the nature of payment),

Chapter 9

whereupon he said: It is to be made on the spot. This is what I heard (from Allah's Messenger (may peace be upon him).
(17) Sahih Muslim Book 010, Number 3877:
Ubaidullah b. Abu Yazid heard Ibn 'Abbas (Allah be pleased with them) as saying: Usama b. Zaid reported Allah's Apostle (may peace be upon him) as saying: There can be an element of Riba in credit
(18) Sahih Muslim Book 010, Number 3878:
Ibn 'Abbas; (Allah be pleased with them) reported on the authority of Usama b. Zaid Allah's Messenger (may peace be upon him) as having said this: There is no element of Riba when the money or commodity is exchanged hand to hand.
(19) Sunan Abu Dawood Book 22, Number 3343:

Chapter 9

> Narrated Ubadah ibn as-Samit:
> The Apostle of Allah (peace be upon him) said: Gold is to be paid for with gold, raw and coined, silver with silver, raw and coined (in equal weight), wheat with wheat in equal measure, barley with barley in equal measure, dates with dates in equal measure, salt by salt with equal measure; if anyone gives more or asks more, he has dealt in Riba. But there is no harm in selling gold for silver and silver (for gold), in unequal weight, payment being made on the spot. Do not sell them if they are to be paid for later. There is no harm in selling wheat for barley and barley (for wheat) in unequal measure, payment being made on the spot. If the payment is to be made later, then do not sell them.

9.3 All these *ahaadeeth* have necessarily to be examined in the Qur'aanic light. We are likely to go astray, as we have already seen in the

Chapter 9

preceding Chapter, if we do not do so. Let me therefore reiterate here that in that divine light, discussed herein above in Chapter 1, *Ar-Riba* is nothing but the injustices or iniquities that human beings are prone to effect in any transactions among themselves.

9.4 As in the case of dates, so in the cases of other products like wheat, barley, gold, silver etc. specifically mentioned in the *ahaadeeth*, enumerated in paragraph 9.2 above. It was to avoid any such injustices that the Prophet had set the norm of 'like for like, hand to hand'. We have discussed the significance of 'like for like', taking the example of dates, in the preceding Chapter. We shall now discuss the significance of 'hand to hand' here in this Chapter.

9.5 'Hand to hand' does of course mean 'on the spot' or 'immediately'. The import of the *ahaadeeth*, in the context of this phrase, is that the exchange of like for like would be devoid of

Chapter 9

Ar-Riba if and only if the exchange takes place, on either side, immediately. In other words, if I had borrowed 1 kg of wheat from my neighbour last week and return the same quantity of wheat of the same quality today, there could still be an element of *Ar-Riba* involved in this exchange, in terms of the *ahaadeeth* above-mentioned! Why?

9.6 Why, indeed! As per the well-established and accepted norms, the exchange would be considered as perfectly all right. And I have not come across any studied analysis seeking an answer to this important question. Does not the Qur'aan say, "—*lakum ruoosu amwaalikum*" [Q: 2.279] and haven't I returned the *amwaal* of my neighbour accordingly? How could there still be an element of *Ar-Riba* in that transaction?

9.7 To understand fully the implications of such a transaction, where a thing borrowed is returned after a lapse of time, let us take another

Chapter 9

example – a macro one. Suppose I am a wholesale merchant dealing in wheat. My stock is exhausted, and my supplier can send me fresh stocks only after a week. In this situation, I get an order from a longstanding valued customer for immediate supply of ten thousand kgs. So, I borrow the quantity required from a fellow trader and honour the order. But the demand for wheat had increased so much that week that the fellow trader who had lent to me found his own stock exhausted midway during that week. He could not therefore honour the orders placed by his own customers. And those regular customers of his had to go to other suppliers.

9.8 Now in this set of circumstances, would not my said fellow trader be put to a loss even if I return to him only wheat of the same quantity and quality after a week? Would he then not be wronged? And Allah says that neither the borrower nor the lender should be wronged [Q: 2.279]. I would indeed, in fact, be inflicting an economic injustice on the fellow trader. I

Chapter 9

would, in other words, be indulging in *Ar-Riba* in terms of verse Q: 30.39.

9.9 The same kind of economic injustice or *Ar-Riba* would be inherent, on a micro level, when I return 1 kilogram of wheat after a week to my neighbour. It is another matter that my neighbour, being a good neighbour, may not at all mind the injustice. But Allah is ever observing me. And if I indeed care for His dreadful warning that takers of *Ar-Riba* would be at war with Him and His Apostle [Q: 2.279], I should return a little more than 1 kilogram of wheat. I should do so even surreptitiously, to avoid my neighbour's good-neighbourly protests.

9.10 This may raise a question in our minds as to how much more one should give in such situations. It is neither necessary nor practical to be exact, in such micro cases. Allah is great — merciful and gracious. He is mindful of our good intentions; He does not mind our honest

Chapter 9

little mistakes, which we are bound to make in such circumstances. But we may see to it that we err on the safer side.

9.11 The *ahaadeeth* enumerated herein above in this Chapter, in the Qur'aanic light, would lead us to the conclusion that if a loan is returned, after a lapse of time, in the same quality and quantity, the transaction may tantamount to Ar-Riba dealing. It is therefore most unfortunate that we have been treating – that too in the name of Islam – such *Ar-Riba* dealings as veritable epitomes of virtue.

9.12 It may well be argued that the said *ahaadeeth* are regarding sale of goods and not regarding goods taken or given on loan. But what really is the difference between the two kinds of transaction? In sales, goods are exchanged on the spot while in loan transactions, there is a lapse of time between the two parts of the exchange – if one party gives the goods to the other party now, the other party

Chapter 9

gives the equivalent goods in exchange after some time. In other words, loan transactions are nothing but sales on credit. And there can be an element of *Ar-Riba* in credit, on the authority of the Prophet himself as seen from the *hadeeth* enumerated as (17) in paragraph 9.2 above.

9.13 There is another interesting *hadeeth* that can be quoted in this connection, although it is not originated with the Prophet. The English translation thereof is copied below:

(20) Muwatta of Imam Malik Book 31, Number 31.43.93:

And Malik related to me that he had heard that a man came to Abdullah ibn Umar and said, "Abu Abd ar-Rahman, I gave a man a loan and stipulated that he give me better than what I lent him." Abdullah ibn Umar said, "That is Riba." Abdullah said, "Loans are of three types: A free loan which you lend by which you desire the pleasure of Allah, and so you have the pleasure of Allah. A

Chapter 9

free loan which you lend by which you desire the pleasure of your companion, so you have the pleasure of your companion, and a free loan which you lend by which you take what is impure by what is pure, and that is usury." He said, "What do you order me to do, Abu Abd ar-Rahman?" He said, "I think that you should tear up the agreement. If he gives you the like of what you lent him, accept it. If he gives you less than what you lent him, take it and you will be rewarded. If he gives you better than what you lent him, of his own good will, that is his gratitude to you and you have the wage of the period you gave him the loan."

9.14 Before discussing this *hadeeth*, let me again point out that it does not purport to convey a saying of the Prophet himself. But it conveys the opinion of Abdulla ibn Umar, a distinguished Companion of the Prophet. As per

Chapter 9

this opinion, stipulation in a loan agreement for the borrower to give to the lender better than what was lent, would be *Ar-Riba*. Let us now examine this opinion in the Qur'aanic light.

9.15 The Qur'aan says, '----you are entitled to get back your capital dues. You shall wrong not, nor shall you be wronged' [Q: 2.279]. So, what the lender is entitled to get back is not only the equivalent of what he lent, but also in addition, the equivalent of what he might lose by the lending. Otherwise, he would be wronged, as in the example given in paragraphs 9.7 and 9.8 above. The two equivalents together, therefore, would be the 'capital dues' of the lender. And 'what was lent', in the *hadeeth* under discussion, would be such 'capital dues', in the light of the Qur'aanic verse. If the loan agreement stipulated that the borrower should give better than such 'capital dues' to the lender, then the excess over such 'capital dues' would be *Ar-Riba*.

Chapter 9

9.16 This interpretation of Abdulla bin Umar's opinion, construed in the Qur'aanic light, gets corroborative support from *hadeeth* # (17) quoted in paragraph 9.2 above wherein the Prophet is reported to have said that there could be an element of *Ar-Riba* in credit. The element of *Ar-Riba* in the example quoted in *hadeeth* # (20) of paragraph 9.13, under discussion, could be the equivalent of what the lender would lose, if he is deprived thereof when the loan is returned.

9.17 The interpretation receives corroborative support also from Abdulla bin Umar's own statement at the end of that *hadeeth*. He is reported to have said thereat that the excess, willingly and gratefully given by the borrower, may be accepted by the lender as the wage of the period of the loan. If the excess were the wage of the period of the loan, then it could not have been *Ar-Riba*; it would be part of his rightful dues, without which he could be wronged as in the example given in paragraphs

Chapter 9

9.7 and 9.8 above. Had the excess or wage been *Ar-Riba*, the lender could not accept it; for, in terms of *hadeeth* at # (10) herein above in this Chapter, the taker and the giver of *Ar-Riba* are both equally guilty.

9.18 From the *ahaadeeth* discussed in this Chapter in the Qur'aanic light, we may draw the following conclusions:
1. There would be no *Ar-Riba* in 'like for like, hand to hand' dealings. This is a sort of a 'standard' set by the Prophet to check *Ar-Riba* transactions.
2. As per this standard, there could be an element of *Ar-Riba* in loan transactions where 'like' is returned for the 'like' after a lapse of time, and not immediately.
3. The loss that the lender may potentially suffer in such loan transactions may constitute the element of *Ar-Riba* therein.

Chapter 9

4. Where loans are taken on personal levels of things which the lenders are not doing business in, it may not be proper for the lender to stipulate additional returns by way of wages for the period of the loan.
5. But it would be a duty upon the borrower to give appropriate additions in return, unless the borrower is in straitened circumstances.
6. Because of such circumstances, if the borrower is unable to return the loan, partially or fully, even after being given adequate extensions of time, the lender should consider waiver of the loan partially or fully as the case may be. He should have faith in Allah rewarding him for the sacrifice.
7. Where the loan, however, is of a thing, in which the lender does his business, the lender is entitled to provide for, in the loan agreement, getting back adequate compensation also for the loss

Chapter 9

he may sustain because of the loan. The compensation would be part of his rightful *amwaal*.

ISLAM & INTEREST

CHAPTER 10
AHAADEETH ON *AR-RIBA* – IV

10.1 In this Chapter let us consider other *ahaadeeth* on *Ar-Riba*, which have their origin in a saying of the Prophet himself. Translations of such *ahaadeeth* available to me are copied below:

(1) Sahih Muslim, Book 010, Number 3863:

Fadala b. Ubaid al-Ansari reported: A necklace having gold and gems in it was brought to Allah's Messenger (may peace be upon him) in Khaibar and it was one of the spoils of war and was put to sale. Allah's Messenger (may peace be upon him) said: The gold used in it should be separated, and then Allah's Messenger (may peace be upon him) further said: (Sell) gold for gold with equal weight.

(2) Sahih Muslim, Book 010, Number 3864:

Fadila b. 'Ubaid (Allah be pleased with him) reported: I bought on the day (of the Victory of Khaibar) a necklace for

Chapter 10

twelve dinars (gold coins). It was made of gold studded with gems. I separated (gold from gems) in it, and found (gold) of more (worth) than twelve dinars. I made a mention of it to Allah's Apostle (may peace be upon him), whereupon he said: It should not be sold unless it is separated.

(3) Sahih Muslim, Book 010, Number 3866:

Fadala b. 'Ubaid reported: We were in the company of Allah's Messenger (may peace be upon him) on the day (of the Victory of) Khaibar, and made transaction with the Jews for the 'uqiya of gold for two dinars or three (gold coins), whereupon Allah's Messenger (may peace be upon him) said: Do not sell gold for gold but for equal weight

(4) Sunan Abu Dawood, Book 23, Number 3534:

Narrated Abu Umamah:

Chapter 10

The Prophet (peace_be_upon_him) said: If anyone intercedes for his brother and he presents a gift to him for it and he accepts it, he approaches a great door of the doors of Riba.

(5) Sunan Abu Dawood, Book 41, Number 4858:

Narrated Sa'id ibn Zayd:

The Prophet (peace_be_upon_him) said: The most prevalent kind of Riba is going to lengths in talking unjustly against a Muslim's honour.

(6) Al-Muwatta of Imam Malik, Book 31, Number 31.39.85:

Yahya related to me from Malik from Abu'z-Zinad from al Araj from Abu Hurayra that the Messenger of Allah, may Allah bless him and grant him peace, said, "Delay in payment by a rich man is injustice, but when one of you is referred for payment to a wealthy man, let him be referred."

Chapter 10

10.2 Let us first take up for our deliberations the first three from the *ahaadeeth* enumerated in the foregoing paragraph. These three *ahaadeeth* are related to the Muslim conquest of Khaiber, a centre of Jews, during the time of the Prophet. The Jews were rich, and the Muslims got a rich booty in gold, silver, jewels etc. The Muslims, being used to a simple way of life, were not accustomed to using the costly articles for themselves. So, they began selling those articles, for cash, to the same Jews. And being unaware of the high value of the articles, the Muslims sold those at a pittance, much below their real value.

10.3 When the Prophet came to know of this, he naturally advised the Muslims against squandering away the booty in that fashion. And it was in this context that the *ahaadeeth*, under discussion, were generated.

10.4 What the Prophet advised was that the gold in the booty ought to be sold for equal weight of

Chapter 10

cash in gold coins and not less. The advice was given primarily for stopping the squandering away of wealth, which the Muslims had got as spoils of a war.

10.5 It would therefore appear to be wrong to associate these *ahaadeeth* with *Ar-Riba*. In fact, there is no mention, at all, of *Ar-Riba* therein. Moreover, the conquest of Khaibar took place before the Qur'aanic verses prohibiting *Ar-Riba* were revealed.

10.6 These *ahaadeeth*, however, came to be related to *Ar-Riba* probably because of another *hadeeth* regarding an address given by one Ubaid b. Samit in a later period after the death of the Prophet. The *hadeeth* in question is the one numbered as (8) in Chapter 9 herein above. Therein Ubaid is reported to have said that he had heard the Prophet forbid the sale of, among other things, gold by gold unless it was 'like for like and equal for equal.' Ubaid is thereafter reported to have added, 'So he who made an

Chapter 10

addition or who accepted an addition (committed the sin of taking) Riba.' The manner of narration of the *hadeeth*, coupled with the controversy reported therein, does obviously suggest that this addition was the opinion of Ubaid, rather than the saying of the Prophet.

10.7 Even so, let us study the three *ahaadeeth* under discussion here in the light of the Qur'aanic verses on *Ar-Riba*. Yes, the things that were being sold at throwaway prices were obtained as spoils of war. The war was not fought for the booty, but for morally just causes. [What those causes were, are beyond the scope of this book and therefore not dealt with here.] The things left behind on the battlefield by the defeated army were claimed (as such things have always been, and even now being, claimed) as rightful spoils of war. And, as was the general practice in those days, the spoils of war were distributed among the

Chapter 10

participants in the victorious army as their just reward.

10.8 So the Muslims' shares of the spoils obtained in the conquest of Khaibar were, so to say, Allah's gifts to them and were therefore their rightful *amwaal*. They were therefore entitled to get the actual values of the shares when those were sold. But, because of their ignorance, they got much less than what they deserved. The Muslims were the wronged party in those sale transactions. The buyers, on the other hand, got much more in value than what little cash they gave to the sellers. The buyers thus sought and obtained increases for themselves in the rightful *amwaal* of the sellers (i.e. Muslims). The buyers were therefore clearly guilty of indulging in *Ar-Riba* in terms of verses Q: 2.279 and Q: 30.39. The Muslims were the victims of that *Ar-Riba*. The *ahaadeeth* in question therefore are rightly considered as related to *Ar-Riba*, notwithstanding some opinions to the contrary.

Chapter 10

10.9 The next *hadeeth* (# 4) in the list in paragraph 10.1 above is an excellent example of one demonstrating the true Qur'aanic concept of *Ar-Riba*. It shows this concept to be a broad one covering even bribery/graft that is so widely prevalent, particularly in developing countries, today. When A bribes B for anything, B gets something which is not his rightful dues or *amwaal*. B would thus be a taker of *Ar-Riba*. And if A gives the bribe to get in return from B something, which A does not deserve to get, then A too would be guilty of taking *Ar-Riba*. Even otherwise, A would be guilty as giver of *Ar-Riba*. A gift given to a friend, purely out of love for him, is of course not *Ar-Riba*, since the gift is given expecting nothing in return from the friend.

10.10 But the gift, given in the example of the *hadeeth* under discussion, was not given purely out of love for the brother who interceded. It was given, maybe, out of gratitude for the

Chapter 10

brother's intercession. The giver may therefore not be faulted for this. However, if the intercessor accepted this gift given by his brother, the intercession could no longer be considered as a brotherly gesture. Maybe the intercessor had no intention, initially, of getting anything in return from the brother, but the purity of the intention got corrupted the moment, the gift was accepted.

10.11 The acceptance of such a gift has been very aptly described as like approaching a great door of the doors of *Ar-Riba*. As discussed herein before in this book, there are many doors to Ar-Riba. Of these, the one approached by the gift-acceptor in this case is great or large, which would mean that the person would get comparatively an easier entry into the sinful realm of *Ar-Riba*. Such a person can be likened to an official of a Government, who has been assigned the duty of helping citizens. The Government pays the official for carrying out this duty and yet the official accepts gifts, in

Chapter 10

addition, from citizens helped by him! The gifts are therefore not his rightful dues or earnings, and the acceptance of such gifts would amount to indulging in *Ar-Riba*.

10.12 Helping a brother is a *sadaqah*, a duty, likewise, enjoined by Allah upon all persons. He (Allah) has promised rich rewards for carrying out this duty. Therefore, it would be improper or indecent for anyone to accept a gift in addition, for such a *sadaqah*, from the brother helped. Once he accepts such a gift, he would develop a taste for enriching himself with material things, which are not his rightful dues. He would then soon find himself deeply immersed in *Ar-Riba* dealings. His entry into the realm of *Ar-Riba* would thus be very easy, as there would be no man-made laws to prevent him from accepting such a gift in the first instance.

10.13 Now, with reference to the *hadeeth* # (5) in paragraph 10.1 above, a Muslim's honour is

Chapter 10

his asset. Any one speaking against it is in effect trying to destroy it. Why does one try to destroy another's honour? There could be several possibilities: enmity, rivalry, envy, hatred or a sheer perverse sense of pleasure one gets by denigrating others. Mind you, such things do happen in real life, and with people who have otherwise a pious exterior! Remember Satan's vow of doing his damned best in misleading humans. Rest assured that it is the handiwork of none other than the Satan himself at his best, when a Muslim denigrates a brother Muslim.

10.14 What really happens then is that the former is unauthorisedly and unjustly expending from the latter's asset, i.e. the latter's honour, for enjoying a dubious, perverse pleasure. The former, in other words, is usurping the latter's *amwaal*. The former therefore is indulging in *Ar-Riba*. And such *Ar-Riba* is the most prevalent and the worst of its kind, undoubtedly.

Chapter 10

10.15 We now come to the last of the *ahaadeeth* – # (6) – enumerated in paragraph 10.1 above. If a wealthy man delays making a payment to someone else, it would be injustice according to the *hadeeth*. And since this would be a transactional injustice, it should amount to *Ar-Riba*, in the light of the Qur'aanic Verses, as we have already seen herein above in this book. But if reverse is the case, i.e. if a wealthy man has to receive payment from someone else who is not wealthy, then the wealthy man is advised to allow more time, if required by the other man, to make the payment. This would be, on the other hand, an act of *sadaqah* on the part of the wealthy man, and an act in the interest of justice!

ISLAM & INTEREST

CHAPTER 11
INSURANCE AND COPYRIGHT

11.1 Insurance is a universally adopted welfare measure. In Life Insurance, for example, a human life is insured for a certain amount of money with Insurance Company. The insured person, or any one else on his behalf, has to pay to the Company a fraction, known as premium, of the amount insured at regular intervals of time. The premium is to be paid, from time to time, for a fixed period. The sum of all the premiums paid during this period would roughly be equal to the amount for which the life is insured.

11.2 Now if at any time, during the period of contract for the insurance, the person, whose life is insured, dies, the beneficiary of the insurance gets the full amount insured from the Company. That is, even though all the premiums have not been paid. This is undoubtedly a welfare scheme to provide for some immediate relief to the beneficiary who would otherwise be put to a financial hardship because of the death of the life insured.

Chapter 11

11.3 Such cases naturally would entail financial losses to the Insurance Company. No Company would be financially viable if it would not find ways and means to make up these losses and in addition to provide for its overhead expenses and for a reasonable profit for itself.

11.4 For this purpose, the Insurance Company invests its funds in shares of other Companies, in Fixed Deposits etc. A part of the income thus obtained would therefore be by way of interest. It is this interest money that some of the present-day Islamic scholars are objecting to. Their argument is: since (according to them) interest is prohibited in Islam, part of the income of Insurance Companies becomes *haraam* (prohibited). And as such, the insurance money given on the death of a person also becomes *haraam*.

11.5 We have seen, at considerable length in this book, that interest, as such, is not prohibited

Chapter 11

in Islam. It would consequently be a falsity to say that under Islam, a welfare measure like Insurance is prohibited. This falsity maligns the fair name of Islam. It is nothing but a man-imposed prohibition, falsely and therefore blasphemously attributed to Allah.

11.6 Now as regards 'Copyright', it is a right, sanctioned by man-made laws in this world, by virtue of which, any original producer, maker, builder or author of a product, whether material or intellectual, is granted exclusive rights over its production. No one else has that right unless permitted by the original producer etc.

11.7 The Copyright law similarly protects an author of a book. No one else has the right to produce copies of the book unless expressly permitted by the author. It is this exclusive right of the author that is branded as un-Islamic in some quarters. Some people believe that the royalties that authors of very popular books unendingly receive would amount to *Ar-Riba*.

Chapter 11

11.8 As we have already seen several times in this book, *Ar-Riba* involves unjust usurpation of other peoples' dues, property or earnings. Does such a thing happen when an author of a popular book goes on receiving benefits there from, year after year, unendingly? Should he give up his copyright to the book, after receiving his dues commensurate with the intellectual efforts he had put in to bring the book into existence? This is the moot question we must examine here.

11.9 In the production and sale of a book, several persons are involved, viz., the Printer, the Publisher, the retail Bookseller etc., besides the Author. The price of the book is fixed in advance, taking into consideration factors like likely volume of sale, adequate returns to the Author and the Publisher, the Printer's charges, the Booksellers' commission etc. Now if the book becomes very popular and the sale figure exceeds expectations, the returns to the Author

Chapter 11

and the Publisher would naturally exceed the targeted expectations. Would such additional returns be tantamount to usurping rightful dues of other persons?

11.10 It is the readers of the book who bear the total cost of the book, ultimately. It would be a case of *Ar-Riba* if any such reader were paying more than the real worth of the book when he pays the price thereof. If the price had been fixed honestly taking the factors mentioned herein above into account, it cannot be said that the reader is paying more than the real worth of the book.

11.11 It may however be argued that when the sale reaches the targeted figure, the Author gets his full dues. The price of the book for its further sale thereafter should be re-fixed deducting the Author's due from the original price.

Chapter 11

11.12 But such re-fixing of the price would be unfair, unjust and impracticable on several counts. It is the Author who gives the greatest contribution to the making of the book. It would therefore be highly improper to deny him any further share in the fruits of his labour, while the other, lesser, contributors continue to enjoy their further shares. Furthermore, it would be a discrimination against the earlier buyers of the book, if copies of the same were sold later at a decreased price. Moreover, when the book has become popular, people would be ready to buy it at more than its declared price. This could lead to black-marketing and part of the buyers' money, in that case, could go into the hands of the real *Ar-Riba* takers.

11.13 The decrease in the price of the book could thus effectively be ineffective. And while the Author gets deprived of what could be a God-given bonus to him, on the dubious premise that it would be *Ar-Riba*, the real *Ar-Riba* eaters would have a field day.

Chapter 11

11.14 It would therefore be illogical artificially to impose a cut-off quantum in the sale of the book, whereupon the Author would not get any share in the profits accruing. In the given circumstances, it would not be logical also to allege that the Author would be seeking to enrich himself in the *amwaal* of the numerous buyers of the book. It would not be logical, in other words, to allege that the Author would be indulging in *Ar-Riba* even when he continues to get his share of profits after the said cut-off quantum. As a matter of fact, it would be more appropriate to say that the Author would be getting a bonus from Allah for his good effort.

11.15 By granting this bonus, Allah Almighty would only be testing the Author. The test would be whether the Author was dutifully adhering to the divine commandments. Allah commands [Q: 2.219] that the riches, which are surplus to one's needs, be spent on the needy and the poor, by way of *sadaqah* and *zakaat*.

Chapter 11

11.16 These conclusions, it may well be noted, are in respect of a book, which does not cater to the baser instincts of a human being. Pornographic books, for example, are outside the scope of these discussions. Income from such books would be entirely *haraam* in the Islamic scheme of things.

ISLAM & INTEREST

APPENDIX - I

1. A cyber-friend of mine had sent me the article copied below. It depicts a different viewpoint. I invite my readers to go through this article as also my comments thereon, which follow the article.

R I B A
By Sayyid Ameenul Hasan Rizvi
Published by Saudi Gazette
(December
23, 1996 / January 4, 1997)

Verses 2:275/276/278, 3:130, 4:161 and 30:39. There is one very important word in all these verses which has been translated quite erroneously by all the translators and the erroneous translation distorts a very important law of Islam. That Arabic word is riba which has been translated by all with the word "usury".

Now "usury", as every English dictionary tells us, means exorbitant or excessive rate of interest. If the word

Appendix - I

"usury" is accepted as the translation of riba it would mean that the prohibition so vehemently forcefully and awe-inspiringly (Allah has permitted trade and forbidden usury 2:275 and O ye who believe, fear Allah and give up what remains of your demand towards usury and if you do not, take notice of war from Allah and His Messenger... (2:278/279) is only for charging (and paying) excessive rates of interest and, conversely speaking, taking and paying interest at a low or reasonable rate is permitted by Allah! Islamic law is clear; it forbids taking any amount, howsoever low and insignificant it may be, in excess of or over and above the principle amount (raas-ul maal, as it is called in Arabic) given as loan, and terms any amount in excess of the raas-ul maal as riba and strictly forbids it.

Appendix - I

In Arabic there is only one word - riba - which covers the English word "usury" and "interest" both. In fact, in English too, the word: usury: is a later introduction. In 17th century when banks (in their early form) started functioning in England, the rate of interest charged by the banks was considerably lower than what was then charged by money-lenders. It was to differentiate between the two the bankers gave currency to the word "usury" in contra-distinction with "interest". But Islam brooks no such distinction and strictly forbids charging any amount over and above the principle even if it be just one halala over ten thousand dinars (the ratio being just by way of an example). Interest in all its varied forms, be it just nominal or exorbitant/exploitative simple or compound, and regardless of the loan being of a consumptive or productive nature, is completely forbidden.

Appendix - I

The translation of the word riba with "usury", may be acceptable only when it has appeared in 3:130 because the word riba is qualified with ad'afun mud'afah "doubled and multiplied", as has been translated by all, which may terminologically be described as "compound interest". But this does not provide any justification for the same translation in the other verses for three reasons: One, that the Verse 3:130 was not revealed to prohibit the Interest but in the backdrop of the reverse suffered by Muslims in the Battle of Uhd (Hijra year 3) it was meant to just create an aversion against worldly allurements. Two, there is no similar qualifying expression in 2:275 wherein charging (and paying) interest, per se, has been categorically declared as haraam (forbidden) "... Allah has permitted trading and forbidden riba..." nor so in

Appendix - I

any other verse (except in 3:130) wherein this word (riba) has appeared. It is, thus, an obvious distortion of the clear Islamic Law to translate the Qur'anic word riba with "usury" as all the translators have done.

Before concluding I would like to revert to the translation of riba with usury as done by all the translators and to make some observations. My feeling is that employing the word `usury' in translating riba is not inadvertent but in deliberate preference to `interest'. The reason, I think, is that influenced by a stream of Western thought, the learned translators also believed that trade, commerce and economy in modern times cannot flourish, or survive even, without the interest-based banking system and other financing institutions. On the other hand, they were confronted with the Qur'an's categorical declaration

Appendix - I

forbidding the taking and giving of interest, further supported by the authentic Traditions of the Prophet (pbuh). They thus found themselves in an embarrassing situation; if the word riba is translated with interest Islam will be branded as an impractical religion sponsoring a stagnated mediaeval economic order with no progress in commerce and industry and flashing prosperity. To wriggle out of this dilemma they thought of `usury' as the translation for riba which restricts the prohibition to excessive and exploitative rate of interest and thus leaves the field open for a moderate rate of interest which the banks and financial institutions claim they charge in comparison with what the money-lenders of earlier times used to charge.

Muhammad Asad was quite conscious of this dilemma and therefore he has

Appendix - I

given a very lengthy explanatory note (No 35) to verse 30:39 (this because surah 30 is earlier to surah 2 and 3 in chronological order of revelation). At one place in the foot-note he says, "considering the problem in terms of economic conditions prevailing at or before their time, most of the early Muslim jurists identified this unlawful addition with profits obtained through any kind of interest-bearing loans irrespective of the rate of interest and the economic motivation involved" (emphasis added by me).

Asad is not right in attributing the above view to most of the early Muslim jurists. That was, in fact, the opinion firmly held by all the early Muslim jurists. Besides what is important to note is that Asad does not give any hint of his agreeing with the 'early jurists' in the matter. On the other hand, his holding a

Appendix - I

contrary view (that it is only the exorbitant and exploitative rate of interest which the Qur'an prohibits) is clearly reflected in his observation in the same foot-note: "The opprobrium of riba... attached to profits obtained through the interest-bearing loans involving an exploitation of the economically weak by the strong and resourceful..." (emphasis added by Asad himself).

I am not surprised so much at Asad, Palmer, Sale, Arberry, Dawood, Pickthall, Yusuf Ali and Irwing committing this error, as I am at Hilali & Mohsin committing it and at finding the same also in the IIIT and Madina (revised) versions of Yusuf Ali's, for which I can think of no explanation. As a Muslim one should hold the firm belief that when Allah has prohibited interest and has declared that He

Appendix - I

deprives interest of all blessings (2:276) it has but to be so. And it is not a mere wishful thinking or a vain boast. Not just for a few years but for some centuries while Islam was in the driving seat the economy was totally free of interest and also flourished in good measure bringing about all round prosperity and elimination of poverty. The ratio of those living below (what in these days is known as) the poverty line to the affluent was much lower than what it is today even in advanced countries with interest-infected economy. There was trade at intercontinental level and after the conquest of Spain, Muslims, started maritime trade even at a big scale - all free of the element of interest. On the other hand, the report of the World Bank for 1995-1996 clearly admits that interest is the main cause of increasing

Appendix - I

economic disparity between the rich and the poor.

Be that as it may, the fundamental point is, and we say without any trace of apology, that Islam basically aims at establishing not a prosperous society but a pious one. Prosperity sans or at the cost of piety is wholly unacceptable to Islam, and we firmly believe that the restrictions of halaal and haraam (permitted and prohibited respectively) as laid down by Islam do not scuttle the growth of economy but greatly help in achieving all-round prosperity.

----

2. Now I feel it my duty to tell my readers why my views are not in conformity with those expressed in the above article. The detailed reasons for the disagreement can be found in the foregoing Chapters. But let me reiterate my

Appendix - I

views very briefly here with reference to what Mr. Rizvi has stated in the above article.

3. Mr. Rizvi says that the Arabic word, Riba, – or, more appropriately, *Ar-Riba* – covers both the English words, 'usury' and 'interest'; but he goes on to say that to translate the Qur'aanic word only as 'usury', is an obvious distortion of the clear Islamic Law. Therefore, in Mr. Rizvi's opinion, not just 'usury' (i.e. interest at unjustly high rates), but 'interest' at any rate whatsoever, high or low, is what in fact covered by the Qur'aanic word, *Ar-Riba*.

4. Mr. Rizvi points out that Banks in their present form started functioning only since the 17th century. It was these Banks who introduced the moderate rates of interest in comparison to the exorbitant rates charged by moneylenders. Prior to the 17th century, it was such moneylenders who held the sway, not only in England but all over the world including Arabia. That this was the position in Arabia too

Appendix - I

at the time of the Prophet Muhammad (*sallalLahu alayhi wa sallam*), is very much indicated in the Qur'aanic verse 3:130 where the faithful have been exhorted not to indulge in exorbitant (double or multiple) gains. So, from all accounts available to us now, charging exorbitant rates for money-lending was the norm at the time the Qur'aan was revealed. To prevent people from indulging in such unjust usurious gains, therefore, was the Qur'aanic injunction on *Ar-Riba* imposed. And yet, Mr. Rizvi categorically states that Islam brooks no distinction between 'interest' and 'usury' and that interest, even if it be just one *halala* over ten thousand dinars, is completely forbidden. Let us now see whether this categorical statement is borne out by Qur'aanic verses.

5. In the Arabic language, '*rubuww*' means to grow or to increase and 'Riba' appears to be its noun-derivative. The Arabic-English dictionary, I have, is by F. Steingass and it gives these meanings of 'Riba': gain in selling; usury,

Appendix - I

usurious interest. It may be observed from the meanings given that while 'usury' or 'usurious interest' is mentioned, the unqualified 'interest' is not. However, it may be assumed that the other meaning given, viz. 'gain in selling', covers 'interest' also, because, interest is after all a gain obtained by selling 'purchasing power' (money) by Banks etc. So, going by the dictionary, 'Riba' connotes gains of different kinds. But does the Qur'aan prohibit all kinds of gains? No! "And Allah has made *'bai'a'* (i.e. business or trading) lawful" (Q: 2.275), it says. It means that 'a normal gain in selling' is lawful. So, it would be misleading to go by the dictionary meanings to ascertain the Qur'aanic concept of *Ar-Riba*. Even man-made Laws give their own definitions of words and terms when it is feared that the dictionary meanings thereof would be misleading. The Qur'aanic Law being Divine and therefore a perfect Law, there ought therefore to be a separate Qur'aanic definition of the prohibited *Ar-Riba*. My grievance against most of our modern Islamic scholars is that they

Appendix - I

have failed to seek and abide by the Qur'aanic definition and have blindly followed, instead, their own equation of *Ar-Riba* = interest. The Qur'aanic definition has been given by Allah Ta'ala, in the very first Verse revealed regarding *Ar-Riba* (Q: 30.39). It reads: "And that which you give by way of riba, so that it grows by means of other people's properties, earnings or dues (amwaal) --- -------" We should carefully take note of what Allah says in that verse. He says, 'that which you give'. 'That' here could be anything: money, any other material thing or even any immaterial thing like advice, services etc. If one gives these things without expecting anything whatsoever in return from the recipients of those things, then it amounts to giving '*zakaat*' i.e. charity. But, otherwise, Allah tells the givers of these things: '*lakum ruoosu amwaalikum*' (Q: 2.279) [i.e. you are entitled to your principal properties, earnings or dues]. If you are a financial advisor to a Company, you may not be giving it any material thing, but you are entitled to due

Appendix - I

compensation from the Company for your advice to it based on your special knowledge, on account of which the Company stands to gain. If you are a businessman supplying certain material things to people, you are entitled to not only the bare cost of the material things supplied but also, in addition, your due profits thereon in lieu of the services rendered by you in making the things conveniently available to the consumers. And suppose you have a row of houses built and have given them to other people to live therein for a limited period. You are entitled to get some appropriate amount as rent, in compensation for your providing the essential necessity of shelter to the people. The rent would cover the normal wear and tear of the buildings as well. When you seek to get such rent, profit or remuneration at reasonable and just rates, you are seeking your own rightful dues and not those of others. You are then within the limits of your own '*ruoosu amwaalikum*'. But if you go beyond such Qur'aanic confines or limits of '*ruoosu*

Appendix - I

amwaalikum' and try to enrich yourself unduly and unjustly on the properties, earnings and dues of others, you would be entering the prohibited area of *Ar-Riba*.

6. If, suppose, the due, justified or rightful remuneration, profit or rent in the examples given in the preceding paragraph, is 100 units of money, and you charge 200 units instead, you would be indulging in *Ar-Riba*. Or, on the other hand, if you were forced to take 50 units only, it would be the other party to the transaction that would then be guilty of committing *Ar-Riba*. This then is the obvious explanation of the verse (Q: 30.39) quoted above. *Ar-Riba*, as per this verse, therefore, is the unjust gain obtained by usurping the rightful dues, earnings or properties of others. There is always the element of injustice involved when *Ar-Riba* is indulged in. This is corroborated by the Qur'aanic verse Q: 4.161, wherein it has been stated that the *Ar-Riba* takers wrongfully usurp the `*amwaal*' of others. Let me repeat: an

Appendix - I

element of injustice is invariably involved in all cases of *Ar-Riba*.

7. Now, let us honestly examine whether this element of injustice is there when a reputed Bank lends money. A big chunk of the interest money would account for the Bank's expenses, claiming which, by no stretch of imagination, anybody can designate as '*haraam*' under the Qur'aanic Law of *Ar-Riba*. The remaining part of the interest money, which would at most be 3% of money lent, could be the rightful and quite justified profit margin of the Bank. As already pointed out in foregoing Chapters, Banking is a business like any other business. And Qur'aan says, `Allah has made business lawful' [Q: 2.275]. By taking its due profit, the Bank is claiming its own dues (*amwaal*). It is not usurping the '*amwaal*' of others. There is no injustice involved. It is not a case of *Ar-Riba*, in terms of the Qur'aan. Why, then, are we knowingly committing a grave sin: calling something as '*haraam*' under the Qur'aanic

Appendix - I

Law, when it is not? We should deeply ponder on the reason given in the Qur'aan for *Ar-Riba*-takers behaving as if under a satanic spell: 'This is so because they say that business (*bai'a*) is like *Ar-Riba*' [Q: 2.275]. Please note that what the Qur'aan says is 'business is like *Ar-Riba*' and not, '*Ar-Riba* is like business'. Are we not likewise saying, 'Business (of banking) is like *Ar-Riba*? May Allah grant us all, the wisdom to see the Truth and may He save us from committing a grave sin.

ISLAM & INTEREST

APPENDIX - II
A CRITICAL STUDY OF IQBAL AHMAD KHAN SUHAIL'S BOOK 'WHAT IS RIBA?'

Title of the book: WHAT IS RIBA?
Name of the Author: IQBAL AHMAD KHAN SUHAIL
Edited by: Zafarul-Islam Khan, Ph.D.
Publishers: Pharos Media & Publishing Pvt. Ltd.,
P.O.Box 9701, D-84 Abul Fazl Enclave-1, Jamia
Nagar, New Delhi 110025 India.
Price: Rs. 180/-
Pages: 198

1. In the second paragraph of the 5th Section of the book, the Author says that a special sort (and not all sorts) of increase is prohibited under the Shariah. He then adds, "In the Holy Qur'an itself neither is there any explicit description of that special sort nor is there any explicit definition of the word riba."

Appendix - II

2. In other words, as per the Author, the Divine Book is not explicit on what it enjoins on the Believers! It enjoins on them a strict prohibition of Riba (*Ar-Riba*, as mentioned in the Qur'aan) and yet it is not explicit about what *Ar-Riba* means!

3. That is too extraordinary a statement for the Believers to believe in. How can they believe this when Allah Himself says elsewhere in that same Book, "Behold how explicit have We made the messages for them!" [Q: 5.75] True, there are some messages in the Book, which are of an allegorical nature (*mutashabihat*) and the meanings of those are not very clear to us humans. But by no stretch of imagination can the messages on *Ar-Riba* be termed as allegorical. These are divine ordinances, which the humans are required to act upon. And how can the humans act upon unclear messages? The Qur'aanic verses on *Ar-Riba* have necessarily therefore to be explicit and clear i.e. *muhkamat* as the Qur'aan itself terms them [Q: 3.7].

Appendix - II

4. A Believer in the Qur'aan cannot therefore but reject the Author's contention outright that the Book is not explicit about what it means by the term, *Ar-Riba*. The definition of *Ar-Riba*, construed by the Author by inference (*qiyaas*) in Section 42 of his book under review, is based on this wrong contention and has got therefore to be faulty.

5. It (the Author's definition of *Ar-Riba*) relies heavily - almost exclusively - on an instance of *Ar-Riba* mentioned by the Prophet (may Allah's blessings and peace be upon him) in his sermon at his last pilgrimage to Makkah. The Prophet did not explain the term, *Ar-Riba*, in that sermon. He mentioned, just to set an example of personal adherence to divine ordinances, that whatever was due to his Uncle Abbas, by way of *Ar-Riba,* was being waived. The details of the *Ar-Riba* dealings of Abbas were not mentioned. Neither are these details mentioned in the Qur'aan. The Author had obviously

Appendix - II

therefore to rely, for the details, on Traditions (*ahaadeeth*) that came to be recorded in writing only after the lapse of more than hundred years after the death of the Prophet. During this gaping intervening period of more than hundred years, the Traditional anecdotes were being passed on from generation to generation only by word of mouth.

6. With this background scenario in mind, we can try to visualise and examine the rationale behind the definition of *Ar-Riba* inferred by the Author. The rationale cannot but be on the lines as follow: 'The all-knowing Creator, Provider and Guide issued a strict injunction against *Ar-Riba* in the Qur'aan without providing for an explicit definition of the term therein. He (Allah) did not think it fit even to provide for the events prompting that injunction to be recorded in writing immediately after their occurrence. And it was left for the Author of the book under review to infer the definition, fourteen centuries later, from the said events

Appendix - II

recorded on the testimony of people who were not direct witnesses thereof. As for the people who lived and died during those fourteen centuries, they were simply left in the lurch, not knowing the true import of *Ar-Riba*; for, the Author says, the definitions given by the *fuqaha* from time to time during that period, were all erroneous.'

7. The absurdity of the Author's rationale is thus self-evident and needs no further comments. I would go to the extent of saying that it would be heresy for anybody to imply that Allah has left His *muhkam* Verses of the Qur'aan, ambiguous. But what is the ground reality? Which Verse or Verses in the Qur'aan give this definition or meaning of *Ar-Riba*? There is a school of thought which asserts that the Qur'aan has not defined any of the terms, like *Ar-Riba*, it has made use of. According to this school, the Qur'aan has used the terms in the same meanings that were prevalent in Arabia at the time of its revelation, and the

Appendix - II

meaning of *Ar-Riba* prevalent at that time was nothing but interest, as we understand this word 'interest' now. The Author has dealt this question of equating *Ar-Riba* with interest at length in his book. He has commendably exposed the irrationality and incorrectness of this equation and I am in complete agreement with him on this point. Let me therefore go back to the Qur'aan to find out what Allah really means by the term, *Ar-Riba*. Allah says, "------and if there is any dispute amongst you on any issue, refer it back to Allah and the Prophet." [Q: 4.59]

8. And it is unthinkable that Allah will disappoint anyone who sincerely does so. He is our best guide and has, for that purpose, bequeathed to us an uncontaminated and immutable book of guidance, the Qur'aan, for all generations of people till Doomsday. And, sure enough, in His inscrutable wisdom, Allah has provided us the solution to our dispute in the very first verse He revealed, in

Appendix - II

chronological order, in the specific matter of *Ar-Riba*. The verse in question is the 39th of Surah # 30 [Q: 30.39]. It reads: *"Wama aataytum minriban liyarbuwa fee amwaalinnasi, fala yarbu indAllah --------"* [And whatever you give for profit (or gain) so as to have it (i.e. whatever you give) increased in the *amwaal* (i.e. the rightful properties, earnings or dues) of other people, then such an increase is no increase with Allah ------].

9. Riba, in Arabic, literally means increase or gain. The above-quoted Verse, Q: 30.39, indicates that it is only a specific kind – and not all kinds – of increase or gain that gets Allah's disapproval. The specific kind is the increase or gain obtained by usurping the rightful properties, earnings or dues of others. This specific kind of Riba has been mentioned as *Ar-Riba* (the Riba i.e. the kind of Riba that had already been mentioned in Verse, Q: 30.39) in all the later revealed verses [viz., Q: 3.130, 4.161, 2.275 etc.] containing that term. So, it is

Appendix - II

this specific kind of Riba that is prohibited in Verse 2.275.

10. It is therefore evident that the phrase, '*Wama aataytum minriban liyarbua fee amwaalinnasi*', of Verse 30.39 defines *Ar-Riba* that stands prohibited by virtue of Verse 2.275. The Author of the book under review has indeed stated that it is only a specific kind or sort of Riba that is prohibited in the Qur'aan, but he unfortunately failed to see the clear and unambiguous definition thereof in Verse 30.39.

11. The Qur'aanic Concept of the prohibited Ar-Riba would therefore, in short, be: "The unjust increase or gain that a party to a transaction contrives or manipulates to get, at the cost of others by usurping the others' rightful properties, earnings or dues." The Qur'aanic injunction against the Riba of this kind obviously aims at eliminating injustice from all kinds of transactions amongst human beings and has universal application. It is not

Appendix - II

restricted to only Darul-Islam or even otherwise restrictive in its scope, as the Author of the book under review would have us believe by following his own inferred definition of *Ar-Riba* given in section 42 of the book. The man-inferred definition cannot stand scrutiny in the light of the divine definition. This Qur'aanic Concept of *Ar-Riba*, or the prohibited Riba, is the basic principle of Islamic Economics. The economy of any nation following this principle should be strong and vibrant.

12. To conclude, I reiterate that although the book under review contains some very useful and valid points, particularly the one exploding the myth of *Ar-Riba* being synonymous with interest, the Author's inference of his own definition of Ar-Riba is faulted on the following grounds:
- It blasphemously presumes that Allah has kept the clear (*muhkam*) verses of the Qur'aan, ambiguous and difficult to understand.

Appendix - II

- The Author has failed to take note of the very clear divine definition of the prohibited *Ar-Riba* in the Qur'aanic Verse Q: 30.39.
- In view of the said divine definition, the Author's inferred definition has no justification to exist.
- It is too restrictive and discriminatory as compared to the divine definition. And, in view of the foregoing compelling grounds, there is no need to examine the inferred definition further. It cannot survive.

ISLAM & INTEREST

APPENDIX - III
COMMENTS ON THE MODERN-DAY INNOVATION OF 'ISLAMIC' BANKING

1. The banking system, which has come to be qualified as Islamic, is only a recent product of as late as the latter half of the 20th century. The epithet, Islamic, should not therefore mislead anyone to the belief that the system has the unquestionable sanction of the Qur'aan and authentic Sunnah. This banking system came into being as a result of the consensus among most Muslim scholars that interest is prohibited in Islam. There are, nevertheless, a few who do not agree. It is an accepted fact of life that the majority is not necessarily right and the minority, necessarily wrong. It is only Allah, who is necessarily right all the time. We have therefore to turn to His book of guidance, the Qur'aan, to seek solutions to all matters of disputes like the one being dealt with in this write-up. Allah says, "----- and if there be any dispute amongst you on any issue, refer it back to Allah and the Prophet." [Q: 4.59]

Appendix - III

2. What is prohibited in the Qur'aan is *Ar-Riba*. The Arabic term literally means increase, gain or growth. However, most of the Muslim scholars today insist that the term is synonymous with nothing but interest, as we understand this English word now. They say so because, as per their learned information, the Arabic term was used only in that sense at the time of the revelation of the Qur'aan. They assume that, whatever is the current dictionary or literal meaning of the term now, the Qur'aan used it in that older, the then current, sense and did not give it a distinct meaning or definition of its own. While making such an interpretation, the scholars forget that the Qur'aan is a divine book of guidance for all the peoples, till the Day of Judgement, and not just for the people living at the time of its revelation. They forget that the Author of the Book would be aware of the changes that the future would bring and make adequate provisions in the Book itself to keep His commandments clear and unambiguous for all times to come. They forget

Appendix - III

the oft-repeated divine assertion in the Qur'aan that "Allah makes clear to you His *Aayaat*". The scholars' interpretation has therefore heretical implications and we should hasten back to the Book to find out how He has made His *Ar-Riba Aayaat* (Verses) clear.

3. As we shall presently see, the Qur'aan does use *rubuw*, the verb form of *Riba*, to mean increase, gain or grow, and the scholars do not dispute that meaning. So, the scholars should agree that, at least in the literal sense, *Riba* connotes the noun forms of the English words, viz., increase, gain or growth. All concerned should also agree that by prohibiting *Riba*, Allah did not intend prohibiting all kinds of increases or gains. It is nobody's case that Allah has prohibited increases or gains made by persons by way of their own lawful efforts like in trading and providing numerous other useful services to mankind. Allah has sanctified the gains made through such efforts; for, the Qur'aan specifically says, "... and Allah has

Appendix - III

made business (*bai'a*) lawful ..." [Q: 2.275]. So, there ought to be a kind of gain (or increase or growth) – other than the gains thus sanctified by Allah – which stands prohibited. And the Qur'aan confirms this when, in continuation of the above-quoted clause of Verse 2.275, it says, "*wa harramu-ar-Riba*" [and *Ar-Riba*, unlawful]. The definite article *Al*, preceding the word *Riba* in this phrase, gives a definite indication that the gain, thereby prohibited, is of a kind mentioned in an earlier-revealed Verse.

4. The 39th Verse of the 30th Surah (Chapter) [Q: 30.39] is the earliest-revealed Verse on this subject. And sure enough, one other kind of gain does stand described there! "*Wama aataytum minriban liyarbuwa fee amwaalinnasi fala yarbu ind-Allah ...*" [And when you give anything for profit (or gain) to get the same increased in the *amwaal* of people, then such increase is not an increase with Allah ...]. The kind of gain described here is the one that is derived from the *amwaal* (i.e. the rightful

Appendix - III

possessions, earnings or dues) – not of one's own but – of others. (Also, please take note of the use of the verb, *rubuw*, in the meaning of increase or gain, in the Verse.) When a shopkeeper sells an article for a price that includes a reasonable net profit for him, this gain is his own *maal* (due) rightfully earned by him for efforts in procuring the article and making it conveniently available for his customers. The Qur'aan therefore has said, "... and Allah has made *bai'a* lawful". But if the same shopkeeper, taking advantage of a situation, crosses the bounds of reasonableness and charges a higher price to corner an unduly large profit for him himself, he would then be extracting extra gain out of the *maal* of his customers and not of his own. He would then be indulging in the kind of *Riba*, so aptly described in the Verse, Q: 30.39, quoted above. And it was this (kind of) *Riba*, which was distinguished, with the prefix of the definite article *al*, in all the later-revealed Verses on this subject and finally proscribed in the Verse, Q:

Appendix - III

2.275. Ponder how "Allah makes His *Aayaat* clear to you"!

5. It is therefore crystal clear that the *Ar-Riba* prohibited by Allah is very well defined in the Qur'aan. It is that unjust gain that a party to a transaction contrives or manipulates to have at the cost of others by usurping the others' rightful possessions, earnings or dues. The contention is therefore patently wrong that the Qur'aan did not define the term and just adopted its meaning prevalent at the time of the revelation of the divine Book. There are reasons to cast doubts on that meaning being 'interest', as we understand this English word now. The divine definition of the prohibited *Ar-Riba*, in any case, does not cover interest per se. When a good, reputable bank lends money on interest, the bulk of the interest charged is made up of the proportionate expenses incurred by the bank on the money lent, leaving only a small reasonable margin of net profit for the bank. The expenses incurred by the bank are the

Appendix - III

bank's own *amwaal*, and so are its reasonable profit margins, rightfully earned in the legitimate business of providing purchasing power to its customers. When the bank recovers its own such *amwaal* in the name of interest, it is not committing the sin of *Ar-Riba* defined in verse, Q: 30.39. The bank would be guilty of committing that sin only if its margin of profit exceeds the bounds of reasonableness.

6. It may thus be seen that equating the prohibited *Ar-Riba* with interest is a fallacy. This fallacy is being turned into a sinful falsity by the Ulema's insistence on this equation despite the clear guidance in the Qur'aan. The whole edifice of the so-called Islamic Banking has been built on this false foundation.

7. And to rationalise the wrong notion of the prohibited *Ar-Riba* being synonymous with interest, it is alleged that interest-based dealings, having no risk-factor involved therein for the lenders (with interests being levied at

Appendix - III

fixed rates), are un-Islamic. The allegation is made because of an improper understanding of the basic Islamic Principle of Economics, on the part of persons making the allegation. This basic principle is laid down in the Qur'aanic edict, *"wa ahall-Allahu al-bai'a wa harramu ar-Riba"* [And Allah has made business lawful and *Ar-Riba*, unlawful]. We have discussed, herein above, the interpretation of the edict by taking the example of a shopkeeper. Through *al-bai'a* the gain you get is your own *maal*, while through *Ar-Riba* the gain you obtain is actually the *maal* of others, unjustly usurped by you. *Al-bai'a* has therefore been made *halaal* by Allah, and *Ar-Riba*, *haraam*. The interest moneys that the banks take, being their own *amwaal* as we have seen above, have got to be determinate and therefore of a fixed nature, at least for a period. The objection about the fixed rates of interest is therefore without substance. The rates of interest do change, however, in accordance with the changing circumstances.

Appendix - III

8. The banks, like any individual or other institution, are entitled to get their own *amwaal*. There is nothing un-Islamic therein. "---- *lakum ruoosu amwaalikum la tazlimoona wala tuzlamoon*" [----- to you, your principal (i.e. your own and not others') *amwaal*; you will do no wrong, and neither will you be wronged], the Qur'aan says [Q: 2.279]. If the banks are not allowed to recover their legitimate expenses and profits, being their own *amwaal,* albeit taken in the name of interest, they will be wronged, and Allah prohibits this too. There is no obligation imposed in the Qur'aanic law to make the legitimate earnings of the banks relative or proportionate to the legitimate earnings of the borrowers from the banks and to make the banks thus to take the necessary risks involved. The Qur'aan, of course, requires that in the event of the borrowers being unable to make the repayments on time, a further time be given to them. The divine law also provides for waiver of loans in genuine cases of borrowers becoming bankrupt [Q: 2.280]. This is what

Appendix - III

good banks do and banks run by Muslims are obliged to do. They cannot be so cruel as to deprive debtors, rendered indigent by circumstances, of even their primary needs of food and shelter, for extracting bank money. The plea that there are no risks involved in the banking business is a sham. No human activity in this world can ever be totally risk free.

9. But Verse Q: 2.280 does not negate Verse Q: 2.279. The need for being charitable towards needy persons does not nullify the fundamental right, granted by Allah, to one's own legitimate properties, earnings or dues. It would therefore be wrong to force the banks to take only proportionate shares in the profits, or the losses, in the businesses of the borrowers and not claim their own rightful dues. Yet, this is what the protagonists of the now prevalent Islamic banks would do. They would, in other words, deny the banks the right Allah has granted them!

Appendix - III

10. This alternative mode of financing, called *musharaka* (equity participation), is moreover not a very practical thing to do. The banks voluntarily buying shares of an established Company to share in the profits/losses of that Company is one thing (and all banks do such a thing), but the banks being forced to have such a sharing arrangement also with business ventures taking loans from them, is quite another. It is a very risky proposition; and if loans are given on this basis without taking adequate care to ensure viability of the borrowers to generate enough profits in their businesses, the banks would be doomed. And to ensure such viability, the banks would have to engage services of experts in all the businesses their borrowers are engaged in, first to examine stringently the borrowers' loan applications and then to oversee proper management of the borrowers' businesses. The banks would then not remain just banks but would be converted into business complexes running various diverse businesses besides banking. The banks

Appendix - III

would then be the proverbial Jacks of all trades, with the very likely danger of becoming masters of none. It is the perception of this danger and of the enormity of the risk involved that has made even the 'Islamic' banks shy away from this *musharaka* mode of funding and resort to other dubious modes.

11. One variant of the *musharaka* mode of financing, called *mudaraba*, is however noteworthy. It is the venture capital equity investment. This is an excellent way of financing entrepreneurs, scientists, engineers etc, with bright ideas of promising projects but with no money at all to implement them, and thus salvaging those ideas for the benefit of the general good. In this mode, a firm or a Company is created and a fund, called Venture Capital, is built up by it. This fund is utilised exclusively to finance such projects. If a project succeeds, profits are shared between the financiers and the executors of the project. If it fails, the financiers bear the financial loss and

Appendix - III

the executors, their labour. Such Companies with Venture Funds have succeeded in the USA and have in turn helped entrepreneurs, like Information Technology Professionals, establish their spectacular successes there. Unfortunately, the Muslim world has not taken to this mode of funding with any enthusiasm although championing its cause from the rooftops. But it cannot be adopted as the sole mode by all the banks. If they do so, the funds at the disposal of the banks would not be available to a substantial and varied section of the general public as of now. Moreover, proper expertise would be required to be able to judge the viability of the entrepreneurs' projects. Otherwise the financiers would be doomed. Such financing would have necessarily therefore to be too specialised a job for any bank to handle it normally. It must be done exclusively by a firm or Company created specifically for the purpose. Banks at best could have a separate arm to deal with such financing exclusively.

Appendix - III

12. Although the above-mentioned two modes are, in theory, the main channels of funding by 'Islamic' banks, in practice however these banks have shown a strong preference for other modes that are less risky. [These banks have thus belied their own 'holier-than-thou' attitude towards the conventional banks.] One such less-risky mode is what is known as *murabaha*. It is just another name for 'buying & selling' or trading. The bank buys the article required by its customer and sells it to him after adding a 'mark-up' to its price. Well, this could be a real service to the customers of the bank, if it could arrange for buying the best article available in the market at the most competitive price and then deliver it to the customer at his doorsteps. It is not being done that way and it cannot be done that way unless the banks have adequate infrastructure to do it that way. To expect the banks to have such an infrastructure is really a tall order.

Appendix - III

13. In practice, what the 'Islamic' banks do is to resort to what is called *bai'a muajjal* mode of financing. In this mode, the article/property required by a customer is purchased by the bank and resold to him on a deferred payment basis, taking a higher total value from him. Such a transaction takes place, obviously, when the customer does not have enough money with him to buy the article/property directly from the market. A conventional bank would have given the customer the money required instead and charged him interest. In effect, therefore, the customer pays the difference in value instead of the interest. For him, it is only a difference in nomenclature if the differential value is equal to the interest money. So, the hard fact of the matter is that the 'Islamic' banks do charge additional money, but not in the name of interest. They have adopted this devious way only to circumvent their wrong notion of interest being synonymous with *Ar-Riba* that is prohibited in Islam. We have seen herein above how wrong this notion is.

Appendix - III

14. There is often a claim made on behalf of this sector of 'Islamic' banks that the returns it gets are higher than what their counterpart of conventional banks gets. This only means that the differential in value that the former obtains is higher in rate than the interest charged by the latter. It is very likely that the former can do so by getting more than what is due to it, i.e. by usurping the rightful *amwaal* of the debtors. In their show of one-upmanship over their conventional rivals, therefore, the 'Islamic' banks may end up committing the same sin of indulging in *Ar-Riba*, to get rid of which they had come up.

15. The 'Islamic' banks resort to some other modes of financing also, like *ijaara* (hire purchase) and *bai'a salaam* (advance purchase) etc. But the raison d'être of all the modes is the same. The 'Islamic' banks, while adopting these various modes, are apparently unaware of the fact that the Qur'aanic injunction on *Ar-Riba*

Appendix - III

puts a limit on the differential value they can take. If they go beyond the limits of their (banks') own *amwaal* and delve into the *amwaal* of the debtors, they would themselves be guilty of indulging in the prohibited *Ar-Riba*. And then if such banks accuse those conventional banks, that keep the interest they charge within the limits of their *amwaal*, of indulging in *Ar-Riba*, the managers of such 'Islamic' banks would be like "those takers of *Ar-Riba* who behave as if they are under the spell of the Satan. That is because they say that (banking) business is like *Ar-Riba*. And Allah has made business lawful and *Ar-Riba*, unlawful." [Initial part of verse, Q: 2.275; the word 'banking' in brackets is added to draw attention to the relevance of the verse to the instant case under discussion.] May Allah guard us all from the Satan.

16. I therefore conclude these comments by distressfully asserting that the 'Islamic' banks

Appendix - III

are far from serving the cause of Islam for the following reasons.

- The justification for such banks is the erroneous belief that Islam prohibits 'interest' as such.
- This erroneous belief is the result in turn of a Satan-inspired heretical belief that Allah has not made His Qur'aanic Verses on prohibited *Ar-Riba* clear, explicit and unambiguous.
- The prohibited *Ar-Riba* is clearly, explicitly and unambiguously defined in the Qur'aanic Verse Q: 30.39.
- This Qur'aanic definition does not cover 'interest' per se, unless it is taken unjustly.
- The Qur'aanic definition is much wider in scope than the simple equation of prohibited *Ar-Riba* = Interest, which equation, besides being erroneous, is restrictive.

Appendix - III

- The 'Islamic' banks are thus unduly obsessed with only – and the very word – 'interest', so much so that even rightful dues taken in that name are considered *haraam*.
- These banks are therefore likely to be blissfully unaware of Satan sneaking in the real prohibited *Ar-Riba* into their own dealings from their own backdoors.

ISLAM & INTEREST

APPENDIX - IV
'SOME PRINCIPLES ABOUT THE RELIABILITY OF HADITHS'
(EXTRACTED FROM IQBAL AHMAD KHAN SUHAIL'S BOOK 'WHAT IS RIBA')
(REFER PARAGRAPH 7.2 HEREIN ABOVE)

(a) *Muhaddithun*, may Allah bless them, have laboured extremely hard in the narration of *Hadith* and have established many principles and methods about the art of narration. They have mentioned about each and every narrator how far he is authentic, quality of his memory, from whom he has narrated, who were his contemporaries and where his narrations stand according to the rules of narration. They have accumulated an unlimited mass of material on the art of narration and the history of narrators. However, *muhaddithun* were human and fallible. It is quite likely that some authentic *ahadith* were not upto their criteria of critical scrutiny and judgement and thus they are not available today or they were considered weak or fabricated *ahadith*. Similarly, it is quite likely

Appendix - IV

that a narrator considered by the *muhaddithun* as authentic and having a good memory, in fact might not be so. Or, in spite of having a good memory, he might have made an incorrect narration and thus a wrong narration could have been included among the authentic ones.

(b) Most of the narrations are derivations [i.e., not quotes of actual words], that is, the actual words of the Holy Prophet (pbuh) have not been quoted in the narration and whatever the narrator understood to be the meaning of the Prophet's (pbuh) words, according to his capacity and capability, he narrated with the best of intention is the saying of the Holy Prophet (pbuh). Now, everyone knows that besides words even the slightest change in the style of delivery can induce a great difference in the meaning.

(c) At times the Holy Prophet (pbuh) gave two different instructions on two different occasions and the two had many words in common but

Appendix - IV

they were of different nature, but the narrator mixed up the two by mistake, juxtaposing words of one instruction into the other instruction. And thus, due to a slight change in the actual narration, the meaning changed completely.

(d) Sometimes the Holy Prophet (pbuh) gave a brief instruction and did not mention any reason for it. Now the listener made up the 'reason' for this instruction according to his mental capacity. As the process of narration proceeded further the narrator's addition became part of the original *hadith*. Then on the basis of the expanded narration, some esteemed persons from amongst the *sahaba* or from the subsequent generation, *tabi'in*, issued a fatwa in a certain case according to his understanding, and after sometime this fatwa also becomes part of the *hadith*. See how far off the mark things go and how much the real meaning is distorted. When *fuqaha* got this narration after it had undergone so many changes, they started

Appendix - IV

logical hair-splitting but they did not make any attempt to enquire about the authenticity of a narration themselves in order to cleanse it of the superfluities.

(e) Sometimes we find a narration which is totally irrational or against the Qur'anic text or against the greatness of the Holy Prophet (pbuh). Such narrations can never be acceptable, however authentic their narrators may be. Instead of attributing such narrations to the Holy Prophet (pbuh), it would be more appropriate to consider them as the misunderstanding of the narrator, for the narrators were, after all human and, however high the status in holiness they might enjoy, there is the possibility of misunderstanding on their part, for all the followers of Sunnah agree that infallibility is an honour specific to the Holy Prophet (pbuh). The belief in the infallibility of the narrators is not an injunction of the Shari'ah. And according to our belief, it is impossible that any order of the Holy Prophet

Appendix - IV

(pbuh) could be irrational or against the words and the spirit of the Holy Qur'an. Moreover, piety and holiness are different from the capacity to comprehend issues, and the ability to convey their correct meanings to others is yet another quality and their combination is not necessarily found in one person. But surprisingly enough, in spite of all this, a mistake in the research of *muhaddithun* or in the wordings of narrators is not considered tenable even if some narrations differ from other narrations or from the verse(s) of Holy Qur'an, and even if the acceptance of such narrations invites objections to the true faith of Islam itself and despite the behaviour of the blessed *sahaba*, may Allah be pleased with them, who did not hesitate to reject such *ahadith*. For example, we all know that when Abu Hurayrah, may Allah be pleased with him, narrated that the dead are punished when the bereaved cry, Mother of the Faithful (*Umm al-Mu'minin*) Ayisha Siddiqah [the Truthful], may Allah be pleased with her, admonished him and

Appendix - IV

reminded him that Allah himself has said, "no one carries the burden of someone else." (6: 164) then how could it be possible that the dead are punished when the bereaved cry, that is, another person is punished instead of the perpetrator of the sins? This can never be the saying of the Holy Prophet (pbuh). In fact, what happens is that while relatives cry in bereavement, the dead person grapples with the consequences of his actions. This is the fact which the Holy Prophet (pbuh) had mentioned. Due to a misunderstanding, the narrator introduced a cause and effect relationship between the crying and the punishment. Several other similar incidents have been described by Ayisha Siddiqah and other *Sahaba*. Now, suppose that a lady like Ayisha Siddiqah, the most learned in *fiqh* among the Muslim women, had not been present there and the narration had been left unchallenged what a blemish it would have been on the face of Islam! By mentioning these incidents it is not intended to make *ahadith* doubtful and reject them as result, and

Appendix - IV

be oblivious of the great treasure that we possess today due to the praiseworthy efforts of the *muhaddithun*, a great part of which is the most correct collection of the sayings and deeds of the Holy Prophet (pbuh) and his actions, and thus destroy a great pillar of our faith. The objective is to be careful before accepting a strange *hadith* as authentic. We should not be content with the principles of narrations only, but, keeping in mind the above-mentioned possibilities, it should be compared with other narratives on the subject with similar meaning or context, and should be considered in view of the Qur'anic verses and wisdom of faith. If a narration is correct according to all these criteria, then who can doubt that it is obligatory?

===========================

www.ingramcontent.com/pod-product-compliance
Lightning Source LLC
Chambersburg PA
CBHW030625220526
45463CB00004B/1413